Beyond
the Music

Beyond the Music

the
Bono
Story

Kim Washburn

ZONDER**kidz**

ZONDERKIDZ

Beyond the Music: The Bono Story
Previously published as *Breaking Through by Grace*
Copyright © 2010, 2013 by Kim Washburn

This title is also available as a Zondervan ebook.
Visit www.zondervan.com/ebooks.

Requests for information should be addressed to:
Zonderkidz, 5300 Patterson Ave SE, Grand Rapids, Michigan 49530

978-0-310-73838-1

Art direction: Cindy Davis
Cover design: Kris Nelson
Cover photo: AP Photo/Manu Fernandez
Interior design: Ben Fetterley, Greg Johnson/Textbook Perfect

Printed in the United States of America

13 14 15 16 17 18 /DCI/ 20 19 18 17 16 15 14 13 12 11 10 9 8 7 6 5 4 3 2 1

For Andrew,
my most essential collaborator.

Contents

Chapter 1

When Love Storms a Stadium

And I know it aches, how your heart it breaks
You can only take so much, walk on, walk on

> "Walk On"
> From *All That You Can't Leave Behind*

The Roar of the Stadium

No matter who wins or loses this football game, the crowd is going to cry.

It has been five months since September 11, 2001, the unforgettable day of the biggest terrorist attack on the United States. One coordinated attack on one morning took thousands of lives and left millions more to mourn.

Five months later America is still struggling to get off her knees. Now a rock band from Ireland is about to help her up.

This band, U2, had been inspiring audiences all over the world for more than twenty years. And on this night, they set up their instruments on the biggest stage America had to offer: halftime at the Super Bowl.

In the darkness of the arena energy surges through the audience like a lightning storm. U2's powerful song "Beautiful Day" has just thundered through the stadium and faded out. Seventy thousand voices are screaming their support.

Then, unexpectedly, a gigantic screen, as long as the stage and as high as the stadium, rises behind the band. The glowing white words "September 11th, 2001" scroll to the sky, followed by the name of each person who died in the terrorist attacks that day.

Later Bono, the lead singer of the band, would admit, "I [couldn't] look at the names. If I looked at the names, I wouldn't be able to sing." So he faces the crowd, his voice burning through the emotion of the night as he sings a haunting lullaby.

Sleep. Sleep tonight. And may your dreams be realized.

Then a cascade of notes from the electric guitar signals the beginning of a new song. The drums and the bass join in to drive the beat.

Muffled by the boom of the sound system and the cheers of the crowd, Bono, the biggest rock star in the world, utters a prayer from Psalm 51:15: "O Lord, open my lips, and my mouth shall show forth your praise."

As the procession of names floats past, Bono calls out "America!" Cheers explode, and Bono runs around the stage that embraces the crowd on the field. And then he

Bono performs during halftime of Super Bowl XXXVI in New Orleans, Louisiana, on February 3, 2002.

Jeff Haynes/AFP/Getty Images

takes the microphone and sings U2's anthem of love and hope, "Where the Streets Have No Name."

The band could play all night and the song would still feel too short. When the screen with the illuminated names falls to the ground, Bono makes the shape of a heart on his chest with his hands. Then the singer opens his jacket and reveals that the fabric of the liner is an American flag. The music surrenders to the roar of the frenzied crowd and tears stream down the cheeks of a nation.

Bono has sung a love song to the wounded hearts of Americans.

The Quiet of the Back Room

Two days before the Super Bowl, far away from huge stages and cheering crowds, Bono had been composing a different kind of love song.

At midnight in New York City, he slipped into a restaurant and made his way to the back room. A diverse group of decision makers, strategists, financial planners, church leaders, and generous donors were huddled around tables. Together they wanted to come up with serious, practical ways to end extreme poverty.

Extreme poverty occurs when a person cannot pay for food, water, shelter, clothing, or health care. Today, there are almost one-and-a-half billion people living in these conditions—many of them in South Asia and Africa. Ending extreme poverty in the world would take a lot of fresh ideas, money, commitment, and prayer. But that was why this group had gathered: they wanted to change the world.

Bono had not come here to make music. He was here to make a difference.

"When you sing," Bono explained, "you make people [open] to change in their lives. You make yourself [open] to change in your life. But in the end, you've got to become the change you want to see in the world. I'm actually not a very good example of that—I'm too selfish, and the right to be ridiculous is something I hold too dear—but still, I know it's true."[1]

This gathering of people fighting to end poverty was part of the World Economic Forum,[2] which is an organization that seeks to improve the lives of ordinary people all around the world. This wasn't exactly the place you'd go to find a rock star. But Bono's heart had been moved by the desperately poor, the people that Jesus called the "least of these." When Bono read the Bible, he found over two thousand verses about poverty. Jesus cared about the poor and reached out to the "untouchables" of his age. "It couldn't be more [obvious]," Bono said, "that this is on God's mind, that this is Jesus's point of view."[3]

And so Bono goes into unexpected places to work with unexpected people. He follows his heart and uses his powerful gift of communication with politicians and preachers, presidents and popes.

It's unusual for a rock star—especially a rock star as well known as Bono—to spend time working for others. "I know how absurd it is to have a rock star talk about the World Health Organization or debt relief or ... AIDS in Africa," he said.[4] But he also knows that when he talks, people listen.

This night in New York City, Bono joined a serious discussion. As a team they would learn from experts, try to understand the issues and the problems, and come up with practical ways to change the world for the desperately poor. The man who sang in front of millions of cheering fans wanted to lend his voice to those who had none.

As a young man, Bono's heart had simply led him to music. But once he was in a band, love came into the room, made itself comfortable, and decided to make some changes. Now love wanted him to move mountains.

Before love took over, though, rage had its day for Bono.

Chapter 2

Steinvic von Huyseman Takes on the Tears

It was one dull morning, I woke the world with bawling

"Out of Control"
From *Boy*

A House, Not a Home

Before the rock star, before the voice, before the music, before the famous name, Bono was Paul David Hewson. He was born on May 10, 1960—the second son of Bob and Iris Hewson.

At the time Ireland, his proud and prized country, was embroiled in a civil war. Catholics and Protestants drew battle lines over differences in what they believed. Before the violence ended, more than three thousand people had died. This time in Ireland's history is called "The Troubles."

Because the two groups of people were so suspicious of each other, they lived in separate neighborhoods and attended separate schools in separate parts of the city. Ireland was boiling over. "I grew up in what you would call a lower-middle-class neighborhood," Bono said. "[It was] a nice street and good people. And, yet, if I'm honest, a sense that violence was around the corner."[1]

Witnessing violence and pain in the name of religion had a lasting impact on Bono. He learned to value the distinction between empty religion and the living God. "We've seen [religious differences] tear our country in two," he said. "You hold onto 'religion' ... rules, regulations, traditions. I think what God is interested in is people's hearts."[2]

Bono's parents, Iris and Bob, got married under highly unusual circumstances, since Bob was Catholic and Iris was Protestant. "No big deal anywhere else in the world but here," Bono commented.[3] Their love for each other mattered more than the differences in their faiths, and they didn't take sides in "The Troubles" that tore Ireland apart. Even at a young age, Bono understood that his family's lack of extreme sides in the religion wars made them different in their neighborhood.

Bono attended a Protestant primary school called The Ink Bottle. Occasionally, when the headmaster looked the other way, Bono and the other students kicked balls over the fence that followed along a river and then chased after them. "It has very good memories for me, that school," Bono said with a laugh.[4]

But the next school Bono attended, St. Patrick's

Cathedral Choir School, didn't hold the same affection for him. "I spent a year at St. Patrick's, not being happy, and basically they asked me to leave," he admitted.[5]

In 1972 Bono moved to a school two bus rides away through Dublin's City Centre. Mount Temple Comprehensive School was Ireland's first coed, nondenominational high school. A school that didn't segregate between Catholics and Protestants was a groundbreaking idea in a society so deeply rooted in religious turmoil. But Bono had grown up in a nondenominational home, and he settled in just fine.

Bono was confident, popular, and full of mischief and fun. But more than anything else he was drawn to music. "I've always heard kind of melodies in my head," said Bono, remembering those early days. "I remember standing under a piano at my grandmother's house, when the keys of the piano were higher than my head. [I remember] pressing down on the keys, and then hearing one note and ... looking for another one to follow it."[6]

Like a puzzle to be solved and a story to be told, the melodies in Bono's head had to be sung. Bono would hear a note and want to—*have to*—find the next in the sequence. Whether he inherited a musical gene from his opera-loving father or received it as a gift from God, Bono had a heart for music and a mind for melody.

In 1974, the Hewsons' world suddenly fell apart. At the funeral of her own father, Bono's mom suffered a massive brain hemorrhage. Bono was only fourteen years old, and his older brother, Norman, was twenty-one. Their mother's abrupt death left a grieving family to clumsily, painfully feel their way through the darkness. "Our mother was gone, the beautiful Iris ... I felt abandoned, afraid," said Bono about this difficult time. "I guess fear converts to anger pretty quickly."[7]

The rooms in the house had become crowded with emotion that none of them knew how to deal with. "It became a house of men," Bono explained. "And three, it turns out, quite macho men — and all that goes with that. The aggression thing is something I'm still working at."[8]

Bono's uncommunicative father tried to keep the family together, but instead of connecting, the three men clashed. Aunts tried to step in, but fourteen-year-old Bono wasn't open to any warmth. His brother Norman was dealing with his own sorrow. "Both of us admitted that we were just angry at each other because we didn't know how to grieve, you see ... because my mother was never mentioned."[9]

Bono's father Bob believed that "to dream is to be disappointed." This went against everything Bono felt in his heart to be true, and he clung to his dreams.[10] In fact he would spend his entire life being driven by big ideas and big dreams.

Belonging in the Village

Even though anger and conflict had taken over Bono's relationship with his family, the connections with his friends were easy and secure. He hung out with a group of boys who referred to themselves as "Lypton Village."

They were a tight gang of creative dreamers. Relying on each other, they found peace, escape, and harmony.

Because of his friends, Bono became more and more aware of his dependence on other people. At first he saw this dependence as a weakness, but eventually he came to understand an important truth. "The blessing of your weakness is it forces you into friendships," Bono said. "The things that you lack, you look for in others." [11]

Lypton Village had a special ritual: they gave each other unique nicknames that bonded these close friends even more. Bono had a number of these names. First, his friends called him "Steinvic von Huyseman." This was soon shortened to "Huyseman" and later modified to "Houseman." Shortly after that, the name changed altogether and became "Bon Murray." This name morphed into "Bono Vox of O'Connell Street," which was abbreviated into "Bono Vox" and finally cut to "Bono." "The only person who ever called me Paul was my father," Bono said later, "so I always associate [that name] with doing something wrong."[12] The shortened name stuck, and so did the friendships.

The Lypton Village gang—Bono, Gavin Friday, and Guggi—became lifelong friends. They were bonded by shared history and a sense of humor. Inspired, imaginative, and often absurd, they colored the world with laughter. "We'd put on performances in the City Centre of Dublin," Bono recalled. "I'd get on the bus with a stepladder and an electric drill. Humor became our weapon. I just [stood] there, quiet—with the drill in my hand."[13]

Bono could be as serious as a professor, but his history of pranks and ridiculous jokes was long and proud. "Once my mates came to wrap my car in tissue paper—the entire car. With dozens and dozens of eggs, [they] turned it into papier-mâché, [sealing] it like in a cocoon of tissue and eggs. And when I woke up, they were firing eggs at me. Only problem was my father woke up!"[14]

While there were plenty of wacky shenanigans, the friendships proved serious and steadfast.

"I remember that whenever it was Guggi's birthday, which is three days after mine," said Bono, "whatever he got from his family, or whatever [he got] in cash, he would split with me fifty-fifty. And he ... taught me one of the fundamentals, which is about sharing ... That's what I remember about birthdays. I remember Guggi's birthday."[15]

Even apart from the Lypton Village friends, when Bono was growing up he spent a lot of time with Guggi's family. Guggi's dad quoted Scripture in a way that made the boys snicker a bit—but at the same time they paid attention. "His father was like a creature from the Old Testament," Bono remembered. "He spoke constantly of the Scriptures."[16] The Bible, with its rich language and wisdom, started to seep in.

If God was sending a message, Bono's heart was responding. "I prayed more outside of the church than inside. It gets back to the songs I was listening to: to me, they were prayers. 'How many roads must a man walk down?'—that wasn't a rhetorical question to me. It was addressed to God. It's a question I wanted to know the answer to, and I'm wondering, who do I ask that to? I'm not gonna ask a schoolteacher."[17]

Boosted by friendship, Bono had walked away from tragedy and conflict toward God. But his journey was just getting started.

Chapter 3

The Drum Kit Saves the Boy

Shows me colours when there's none to see,
Gives me hope when I can't believe

"The First Time"
From *Zooropa*

Answering the Call

Before there was music in the rock star's life, Bono just had whispers of melodies in his head. Maybe he could plunk out a few notes on a piano or pluck his brother's guitar. Maybe he could even piece together a poetic verse with a melody. But more often Bono would want to say something and have no fitting way to express it.

Then in the fall of 1976, a notice was posted by a fourteen-year-old drummer named Larry Mullen on the bulletin board at the Mount Temple Comprehensive School. Larry was looking to start a band.

"You have to go," one of Bono's friends said. He got Bono on the back of his motorcycle and together they sped to 60 Rosemount Avenue. Once there, Bono greeted Larry and followed him inside to the "studio" which was actually the kitchen. Little did Bono know that one day he and Larry would be the lead singer and the drummer of one of the biggest bands in the world.

"Larry is in this tiny kitchen, and he's got his drum kit set up," Bono recalled. "And there are a few other boys. There's Dave Evans—a kinda brainy-looking kid—who's fifteen. And his brother Dik—even brainier-looking—who's built his own guitar."[1]

They were joined by another teenager named Adam Clayton, who, Bono said, "was the oldest, and he looked the most professional. He arrived with a bass guitar and a bass amp, and he looked incredible."[2]

When Bono took in the scene, excitement coursed through him like electricity running through a wire. "Larry starts playing the [drums]," he remembered. "It's an amazing sound, just hit the cymbal. [Dave] hit a guitar chord which I'd never heard on electric guitar."[3]

This was the calling that Bono's heart and mind had been waiting for without even knowing it. To develop melodies, to work together with friends on songs that had always moved him, to communicate through music—for Bono it was "the open road." His dreams just got a whole lot bigger.

Their first rehearsal made an impression on people in the neighborhood just as much as on Bono. "Kids started coming from all around the place—all girls,"

Bono recalled. "They know that Larry lives there. They're ... screaming; they're ... climbing up the door. [Larry] was completely used to this, we discovered," Bono laughed.[4]

In the world of rock and roll music, this enthusiasm from fans was a good sign. Their band just might have a future.

The experience of making music was fun, exciting, and new. But to Bono it meant even more than that. "What's interesting is in the months leading up to this, I was probably at the lowest [point] in my life," Bono said later. "I was feeling just teenage angst. I didn't know if I wanted to continue living—that kind of despair. I was praying to a God I didn't know was listening."[5]

Inspired Collaborations

After a few weeks of rehearsing, the band of Bono, Larry, Adam, and brothers Dave and Dik decided to name themselves "Feedback." This name came at least partly from the shrill sound coming back through the amplifier when they played.

At first, they played songs from the radio and records. Unfortunately, the versions Feedback played didn't sound much like the originals. At this point Feedback had much more desire than ability.

Plus, Adam had been keeping a secret. "He had all the musician talk," Bono said. "He looked funky, he acted funky. We didn't realize at the time he couldn't play a note!" he laughed. "And so big was his bluff that we looked pretty much everywhere else to why we were sounding so [bad]. Him!"[6]

When they started out, the band experimented with format as much as music. Although it often felt aimless and accidental, they found their way. "I thought I'd be a lead guitar player actually," Bono said. "In fact everyone wanted to play guitar, as far as I remember. Even Larry, he was getting bored behind the drum kit and he thought, 'Yeah, I'd quite like playing guitar.' Then they stopped me playing lead guitar. Then I was on rhythm guitar and then they stopped me playing rhythm guitar. Eventually I think they wanted me to manage the group, but I wouldn't leave the stage . . . So I began as a singer."[7]

The experimentation didn't stop there. They tinkered with other ingredients as well. Bono suggested adding two girls to mix it up a bit. But the girls' first suggestion was to get rid of Bono, so that was the end of that![8] They also tinkered with the band's name, changing it for a while to The Hype. But ultimately that didn't stick either.

When they tinkered with the playlist, they actually stumbled upon something that made a big difference. They found it easier to perform their *own* material. "One of the reasons we wrote our own songs is because we couldn't play other people's. We were worse than your average wedding band. But we could do *our* thing better than anyone else in the world."[9] The band scrapped the idea of playing cover songs entirely. Finally, Bono had the perfect place for his own melodies.

"If you wake up in the morning with a melody in your

head, as I do," he explained, "it's all about how much you compromise that melody to take it out of your head and put it into music.... Had I not got [Dave] close by, who was an extraordinarily gifted, complex musician, I would be hopeless. Had I not got Larry and Adam, these melodies would not be grounded."[10]

As the group's music found its groove, so did their friendships. "I'd say Larry and I were pretty close friends," Bono said. When the band was on tour, they usually shared a room, where their different styles came to light immediately. Larry was always very clean and organized. He would even bring his own sleeping bag to hotels out of concern that the bed sheets were dirty. Bono, however, was the opposite. He didn't mind if there were clothes on the floor or dirty sheets on the bed.[11]

Different or not, Larry and Bono shared a friendship that came from both loyalty and tragedy. Four years after Bono lost his mother, Larry lost his own mom in a car accident. Similarly they were both then raised by strict fathers.[12] Bono had endured the same grief and struggle as Larry, and he refused to let his friend go through it alone. When the drummer wanted to withdraw, Bono went to Larry's house, made it clear he knew exactly what was going on and how it felt. This shared experience helped the outgoing Bono and the reserved Larry forge a lasting, unique bond as teenagers.

But Larry wasn't the only friend Bono made in Feedback. He also became close to Dave Evans, who played the electric guitar. Before too much time had gone by, Bono called Dave "The Edge," a nickname that never left. Sharing a sense of humor, Bono and The Edge entertained themselves with silly escapades and clever high jinks. And sharing a deep love of music, they knit lyrics and sounds together in great collaboration.

The uncommon circus life on a stage helped to bond the group instead of tearing it apart. "The thing about being in a band is that you've already got a bit missing," Bono explained later. "You know you're not complete without other people." [13]

The relationships weren't easy, but they were worth it. "It's almost impossible to stay in a relationship for your whole life ... but when you do there is such a force. And when we walk onto stage together, *I* have the hairs on the back of my neck stand up." [14]

Within thirty days of climbing on the back of the motorcycle to play music in a kitchen, Bono made another move, just as bold as joining a band. He asked out a girl he knew from school, Alison Stewart (or Ali for short). "It was a good month," Bono grinned later. "I met the most extraordinary woman, and I couldn't let her go. At the heart of my relationship is a great friendship." [15] Six years later on August 21, 1982, with band member Adam Clayton as his best man, Bono and Ali were married in Dublin.

Music's power, possibilities, messages, and melodies sustained Bono. Out of the music sprang laughter and loyalties, big ideas and big dreams. "That's ... the key to all the important doors in my life," Bono explained, "whether it's the band, or whether it's my marriage, or whether it's the community that I still live in. It's

Ebet Roberts/Redferns/Getty Images

Bono and his wife, Ali Hewson, backstage at the U.S. Festival at San Bernardino.

almost like the two sorts of sacraments are music and friendship."[16]

The Open Road

When Bono was still in school, he earned some extra spending money by working at a gas station. While he pumped gas, his thoughts drifted back to the band and their practice sessions. Those rehearsals meant everything to Bono. The clang of a cymbal, the beat of the bass, and the riff of an electric guitar moved him in ways he could hardly express.[17]

But how far could passion and enthusiasm really take a band of teenagers?

"Our talents weren't really the obvious ones that you need for this particular journey," Bono admitted. "But it turned out we had other [talents], which were maybe more important." There was something original about the group's point of view, even if they didn't always express it very well. And they were relentless.[18]

"Our first show was really, really good. And then the next twenty-five were utterly [terrible]," Bono admitted. But the glimpse of their powerful chemistry on stage sustained them, and they recognized what was possible "if only we could play in tune and in time."[19] Even if the group didn't have much experience or very good musical technique starting out, the band members could gain both of those things. With endless hours of playing, practices, run-throughs, and rehearsals, they improved. On the other hand some parts of making music couldn't be learned, bought, copied, or faked. They either had it — an indescribable quality that people connect with — or they didn't. According to audiences, they had it.

"Sparks go off when we play in a room," Bono said frankly. "There's a kind of magic. I remember bands that were much better than us at the time. Technically they looked better. We used to have an expression. We used to say, 'They have everything, but *it*.' We had nothing, but *it*."[20]

Usually, Feedback performed in their school gym.

But in 1978 they got the chance to show their raw promise to a larger audience. On St. Patrick's Day that year they won a talent show in Limerick, Ireland, and walked away with five hundred pounds (about seven hundred fifty dollars) and studio access to record a demo for CBS Ireland. Winning this contest confirmed what Feedback had already suspected. They had "it."

Three days later Dik Evans, Edge's brother, decided that it was time for him to leave the band and move on to other activities. After he played his last gig with the group, Bono, Edge, Larry, and Adam decided to make one more change. Without Dik they weren't really Feedback anymore. The band needed a new name.

After playing around with different ideas, an album cover designer named Steven Averill came up with the name U2. The band agreed. Bono admitted later he didn't always like it. Did it refer to a submarine, a spy plane, or a peace movement? "It's just I never thought about it as in ... 'you too,'" he smiled. "I really didn't, but that's me." [21]

Regardless of Bono's misgivings, the name was fixed. As U2, Bono, Larry, Adam, and Edge wrote and performed hundreds of songs on thirteen albums over the next three decades.

But before all the albums and concerts, U2 followed the rugged road that every new, young band started on. They made the most of every little opportunity and worked hard for every shred of press and exposure. They recorded their first demo tape, gave their first interview in *Hot Press*, and played their biggest gig for a whopping fifty pounds (about seventy-five dollars).

Bono thought he knew a way to help get the band recognized outside of Ireland, but first he needed some extra money. Fifty pounds split between four band members didn't go very far! Bono borrowed money to go to London. As long as the money lasted, he visited record companies and music magazines around the city to drop off tapes that U2 had recorded.

About the same time, the band played extra concerts at home in Ireland. Usually they played in clubs in the evenings, but they decided to take a break from the nighttime concerts. Instead, U2 gave six afternoon concerts in Dublin. Their audience grew almost instantly. Young music fans loved the live U2 summer concerts. And U2 loved their home crowd.

At the end of 1979, the band released their first single, "Three." They watched it rise on the Irish charts. As it rose, they were invited to film a concert for television in Cork Opera House, the biggest concert hall in Ireland.

Momentum continued as Bono's music tour in London started paying off. All of a sudden Britain was calling. Bono, Larry, Adam, and Edge borrowed three thousand pounds (about forty-five hundred dollars) from their families and friends. They packed their suitcases (and Larry's sleeping bag) and headed across the water to England. It was the first time the band had ever played a show outside of Ireland, and they spent two weeks performing in the clubs there.

Casual concert goers were becoming dedicated fans,

following the band from one gig to the next. Plus, the band members were becoming skilled musicians. The music they made was matching their passion. Even though the band was still just earning fifty pounds for every concert they played, Bono felt richer than ever.

"Wherever I feel more myself, wherever I feel the inspiration is, I want to be," Bono said. "So, in my case, being in a band, I feel completely free." [22]

Chapter 4

The Back Door to Heaven

The road refuses strangers, the land, the seeds we sow
Where might we find the lamb as white as snow

"White as Snow"
From *No Line on the Horizon*

When Love Takes Over

The lyrics, the beat, and the hard-driving sound of the band cleared out Bono's heart — a heart that had been crowded with bitterness and anger — and opened it up to love. It grounded him in his relationships and channeled his raging energy into writing music and performing on stage. All of the burning emotions and questions that had been bottled up in his heart could now flow out in full expression. "Rock 'n' roll is not about playing the right notes," Bono said. "It's about a feeling inside you that you want to get out."[1]

The music U2 was making wasn't just aimless musings or random reflections. For Bono, the songs were actually prayers. He found himself in music that tried to understand and describe humanity's relationship with God, whether that was a relationship of anger or of praise.[2]

The music helped Bono process the relationship he had with God. As he explored God's unfailing love, he wrestled with loving others and loving the world. Bono was hesitant to call himself a Christian. "[I struggle] to approach that word," he admitted. "I don't feel worthy to use the word 'Christian' because I know too much about myself. I'd be ... the one who'd just stick my hand out to grab at the hem of [Jesus'] robe," Bono said.[3]

As he explored the wisdom of the Scriptures, Bono found a Christian group in Dublin that fed him spiritually as well. The group's name was Shalom, which means peace. Shalom had no ties to a specific church. Having grown up during "The Troubles" and knowing the history of their divided country, the group was intentionally neither Catholic nor Protestant. Instead they believed God was above church divisions. Bono, along with Larry and Edge, found harmony and strength in the community of believers.

"People who had cash shared it. They were passionate, and they were funny, and they seemed to have no material desires," said Bono. "Their teaching of the Scriptures reminded me of those people whom I'd heard as a youngster with Guggi."[4]

Shalom showed how love could open people up. They

lived as a community, dependent on each other for material things and dependent on God for his grace.

"At that time ... I lived with no possessions," Bono explained. "We were part of a community. Everyone helped each other out, sharing what little money we had. It was like a church that was really committed to changing the world, really. Not in a gigantic way but in small ways: individual by individual." [5]

Bono lived simply and strictly. He learned more about the Bible and other Christian writings. He listened as a respected leader of the Shalom community opened up the Bible and answered some of life's many questions. He learned a great deal about the Bible, coming to understand that the teachings of Christ were more than just words. They held the greatest Truth the world has ever known. [6] Excited about God and excited about the future, Bono told the leader that when the band made it big, they would be able to help the community financially.

But the leader's reaction took him by surprise. He just looked at Bono and laughed. Bono was hurt and confused, and asked what was wrong. "I wouldn't want money earned that way," the leader said.

Bono didn't understand. "What do you mean by that?" he asked.

The leader explained that even though he knew Bono, Larry, and Edge were in a rock group, he didn't approve of the music they were making. He didn't really believe that music was an essential part of who they were. He said that music should only be used to evangelize. As he spoke, Bono realized that this leader didn't understand what the group was trying to do. The band was trying to explore the relationship between God and his people, not tell people what to believe and how to believe it.[7]

Bono, Edge, and Larry knew that they had come to a crossroads. Was the Shalom leader right? Did a commitment to God mean that they couldn't play rock music? Would certain works get them closer to heaven? Would a Mohawk or earrings keep them farther from it? For these three serious believers, the questions had to be answered so they could commit to a band. Or to God. Or to both.

Eventually they each came to a realization. "Where are these gifts coming from?" they wondered. "[Our music] is how we worship God, even though we don't write religious songs, because we [don't] feel God needs the advertising."[8]

One by one all three friends made the personal decision to break away from the Shalom group. Bono admitted it was hard to leave. Years later Bono remembered, "We were just really curious ... and the stuff that I picked up in that intense period of time, I'm still living on."

The bandmates didn't have trouble reconciling the Bible's teaching with the music they played. *Other* people did. But U2 wasn't trying to satisfy other people. The only one they really wanted to please was God.

Love Explained

To some people, it seemed strange that a rock star loved God, believed in the Bible, and sang prayers to an audience of thousands. "It was certainly incongruous to see a rock 'n' roll band down the back of their tour bus with their heads in the back of the Bible," Bono commented.[9] But because of the amazing love of Christ, Bono did just that. In 2006 Bono sat down with a reporter and explained exactly what God's love meant to him.

"My understanding of the Scriptures," said Bono, "has been made simple by the person of Christ. Christ teaches that God is love ... Love [is] a child born in straw poverty, the most vulnerable situation of all, without honor. I don't let my religious world get too complicated. I just kind of go: Well, I think I know what God is. God is love, and ... I respond in allowing myself to be transformed by that love and acting in that love. That's my religion. Where things get complicated for me, is when I try to live this love. Now that's not so easy.

"There's nothing hippie about my picture of Christ," Bono continued. "The Gospels paint a picture of a very demanding, sometimes divisive love, but love it is. I accept the Old Testament as more of an action movie: blood, car chases, evacuations, a lot of special effects, seas dividing, mass murder, adultery. The children of God are running amok, wayward. Maybe that's why they're so relatable. But the way we would see it, those of us who are trying to figure out our Christian conundrum, is that the God of the Old Testament is like the journey from stern father to friend. When you're a child, you need clear directions and some strict rules. But with Christ, we have access in a one-to-one relationship, for, as in the Old Testament, it was more one of worship and

Bono at London's Lyceum.

© Philip Grey/Lebrecht Music & Arts/Corbis

awe, a vertical relationship. The New Testament, on the other hand, we look across at a Jesus who looks familiar, horizontal. The combination is what makes the Cross.

"It's a mind-blowing concept," he continued, "that the God who created the universe might be looking for company, a real relationship with people, but the thing that keeps me on my knees is the difference between grace and karma. You see, at the center of all religions is the idea of karma. You know, what you put out comes back to you: an eye for an eye, a tooth for a tooth, or in ... physical laws, every action is met by an equal or an opposite one. It's clear to me that karma is at the very heart of the universe. I'm absolutely sure of it. And yet, along comes this idea called grace to upend all that 'as you reap, so you will sow' stuff. Grace defies reason and logic. Love interrupts ... the consequences of your actions, which in my case is very good news indeed, because I've done a lot of stupid stuff ... But I'd be in big trouble if karma was going to finally be my judge. It doesn't excuse my mistakes, but I'm holding out for grace. I'm holding out that Jesus took my sins onto the cross.

"The point of the death of Christ is that Christ took on the sins of the world, so that what we put out did not come back to us, and that our sinful nature does not reap the obvious death. That's the point. It should keep us humbled. It's not our own good works that get us through the gates of heaven."[10]

Living by grace and resting in the knowledge that Christ's death on the cross had already saved him, Bono was ready to take on the world.

Chapter 5

Limo Ride to the Circus

She is liberty, and she comes to rescue me
Hope, faith, her vanity

"In God's Country"
From *The Joshua Tree*

Embracing the States

The 1980s found U2 speeding to wide new horizons, playing to larger audiences, and pushing their musical boundaries. In March 1980, Island Records, a major record label, joined the band's adoring audience and signed them to an international deal.

When the band's first album, *Boy*, was released, U2 hit the road. They booked fifty-six shows in the United Kingdom and traveled to continental Europe to perform for the first time. In December they went even further, taking their live show to the United States.

U2 had good reason to believe their soulful rock would appeal to America. America certainly appealed to Bono. For him, it was more than a country. It was a philosophy. "Everybody who values freedom, [forward] thinking, [and] innovation has a stake in America," Bono said. "The country [Americans] may own. But not the idea."[1]

Bono was ready to embrace the United States. The band flew into New York for a two-week tour.

The glittering city, the bustling traffic, the loud street talk all added to the buzz. (The excitement of this visit would inspire the song "Angel of Harlem" that appeared on their album *Rattle and Hum* eight years later.) To add to the thrill of the big city, the band's manager, Paul McGuiness, arranged a surprise: a limousine ride to the hotel.

"So here we were with no money," said Bono, "and [Paul] got the record company to do a *limousine!* Now, we'd never been in a limousine, we'd never been in New York, we'd never been in America. It was mind-blowing. So we all climb into this ridiculous-looking car with Christmas lights around the windows, and we're sitting there, laughing and giggling."[2]

When they finally settled into their hotel, Larry unrolled his sleeping bag onto the bed and promptly fell asleep. Bono couldn't sleep though and turned on the TV. The first program he saw had a televangelist preaching. In the flickering light of the screen, Bono sat and stared at the preacher.[3] He saw the people on the screen speaking his language, quoting the Bible. And yet something about it was all wrong. The televangelist sounded like a robot programmed to speak words without knowing their meaning.

Bono was a believer. He understood the power of the Scriptures the televangelist was quoting. He believed in the healing power of faith. And the words the preacher was speaking sounded very similar to words that Bono himself used about God and the Bible. But Bono felt that he was seeing those words belittled and misinterpreted. As he watched, he remembered the story about Jesus turning over the tables of the moneylenders in Jerusalem's temple. Bono thought that the preacher on television was just like those moneylenders, motivated by greed. He and the other televangelists were trampling on the most precious thing of all: God's love. Instead of bringing their viewers and listeners closer to faith, they were turning people away from God.[4]

This experience angered Bono. He worried that if he used Christian language in America, people would think he was just another televangelist. To him, that would be a tragedy he couldn't live with.

Up the Charts

U2 returned to America when their album *Boy* was released in the United States. Charged up with good reviews, the trip was considerably longer than that first two-week stay.

The schedule was filled with interviews, press, promos, and sixty high-energy performances. During

Virginia Turbett/Redferns/Getty Images

U2 performing live onstage during the Boy Tour in 1980.

free moments, Bono wrote lyrics and composed melodies to get ready for the next album. They had already booked a studio to record new songs, and the schedule was packed. But during a U2 performance in Portland, Oregon, Bono's case of musical notes was stolen.

The loss was devastating. Not only did the band have to start over with entirely new material, but the bill for the studio still had to be paid. They would have to start recording as scheduled, even though they had no music.

"I remember the pressure [the album] was made under," Bono said later. Sometimes he wrote lyrics to songs while he stood at the microphone. At fifty pounds (about seventy-five dollars) per hour for the studio, they couldn't afford to waste a minute.

Nevertheless, the album came together. "The ironic thing about *October* is that there's a sort of peace about the album, even though it was recorded under that pressure," Bono said.

Every time Bono returned to Portland for a concert he asked the audience for any information about that stolen briefcase and the music notes that were inside it. Finally, twenty-three years after losing the notes, a woman found the briefcase in the attic of a house she was renting. She returned the notes to Bono, who called the incident "an act of grace." [5]

In *October,* their second album, U2 covered new territory. The tracks highlighted piano, pipes, Larry's drums, and Adam's bass. Fans of *Boy* were surprised at the new sound, and reviews were mixed. But Bono appreciated the band's fearlessness for trying new things. "A lot of people found *October* hard to accept at first," Bono said. "I think [the album] goes into areas that most rock 'n' roll bands ignore."

Much of Bono's inspiration, writing, and melodies maintained a sense of grace. The band usually sketched out song ideas through hours of sweat and fierce argument, but sometimes the harmony of the teamwork came together with inspired mystery. Bono felt personally moved by one song in particular. Without even realizing what he was writing about, he composed "Tomorrow." Listening to it later, he realized that the song was about his mother's funeral.

But only rarely did creating songs come easily. "If you know what *great* is, you know you're not it," Bono pointed out. "So you have to set up the opportunity to bump into it ... That's why songwriting by accident is so important, and ... getting to the place where that can happen, or as we say, getting to the place where God can walk through the room."[6]

U2 marched on with their third album, *War.* As they explored new ground with political messages, it became their first number-one album in the United Kingdom. Audiences responded to the songs and the stage shows where Bono waved white flags. "Though our [record] is called *War,*" Bono said, "the theme is very much surrender."[7]

To communicate the songs better, Bono knew the performances mattered enormously. As the front man of the band, Bono intentionally looked for a moment or a defining picture for people to respond to and grasp at a show. "It's like when you're writing," he explained, "you're looking all the time for the right image. Or when you're performing, you're looking for those moments." Bono was never content with the distance between the crowd and the stage. He was always trying to cross that distance with the audience—both mentally and physically.[8]

A month after their War tour ended, U2 was named Band of the Year by *Rolling Stone* magazine. By their fourth groundbreaking album, *The Unforgettable Fire*, U2's audiences had outgrown small clubs. They headlined their first stadium show in front of a home crowd at Dublin's Croke Park.

Larry Mullen Jr., Bono, Adam Clayton, and The Edge, of the Irish rock band U2, pose in Dublin, April 17, 1980.

Assessing the music scene, *Rolling Stone* magazine weighed in again: "For a growing number of rock-and-roll fans, U2 has become the band that matters most, maybe even the only band that matters."[9] This time it named U2 the Band of the '80s.

Around the Corner

In July 1985 U2 joined a number of other artists to play Live Aid, a unique concert event for a greater cause. In a series of concerts broadcast all over the world, the "global jukebox" raised money for famine relief in Ethiopia. This blend of music and charity affected Bono deeply. "The thing that I'm most proud of being a part of is Live Aid," he said, "being there, actually seeing music [not only] makes a difference in people's lives but actually saves lives. It was something I'd always felt, but I'll never really recover from." [10]

One hundred seventy thousand people saw the shows live. Four hundred million viewers across sixty countries caught it on TV. For bands, it was a major opportunity to showcase their music as well as encourage people to reach out in charity.

U2 played Live Aid at London's Wembley Stadium to seventy-two thousand people. The band had prepared a set of three of their biggest hits. After "Sunday Bloody Sunday" got the huge crowd shouting and dancing, Bono said in the microphone, "We're an Irish band. We come from Dublin, a city in Ireland. Like all cities, it has its good; it has its bad. This is a song called 'Bad.'"

Looking out at the crowd as he sang, Bono saw a young woman being pushed up against the front railing. He gestured for help but the ushers didn't respond. Unexpectedly Bono had a meaningful moment. The singer leapt over a barrier, jumped ten feet down to the crowd, and motioned to the guards to pull her over the fence. Bono embraced the young woman in a short dance as the confused band, unable to see what was happening off stage, continued to play. The song stretched to fourteen minutes.

The strict time for U2's set ran out without the band performing their last song. Bono's exit from the stage drained the time away, and the other band members could only watch. Larry almost stopped playing altogether. Years later, he joked that he thought Bono had gone out for tea and left them on stage.

Thinking the show had been a failure, Bono was devastated, certain that he had been responsible for what had gone wrong. "I wanted to find that moment," he said. "I got a terrible time from the band ... This was a big show for [us]. There were a billion people watching, and we didn't do our big song. Everyone was very annoyed with me, I mean, *very* annoyed." [11]

As it turned out, however, the event that seemed like a mistake played out on the news as the "breakthrough moment" for U2. The image of Bono dancing with a fan became the key picture for the entire Live Aid event. Audiences had witnessed the emotional and physical connection that the entertainer could make with an audience.

Their reputation as superstars on the live stage was cemented.

Chapter 6

Memories Tattooed on the Heart

Oh, don't sorrow, no don't weep
For tonight, at last, I am coming home

"A Sort of Homecoming"
From *The Unforgettable Fire*

Searching for Mercy

Moved by the experience of playing the Live Aid concert, Bono felt inspired to go to Africa and see in person the realities of life there. He couldn't get the thought of those suffering in Ethiopia out of his head. So he talked to his wife. "We have to try and do something," he told her. "In a quiet way." Ali agreed, and the couple decided to go to Africa. They didn't tell anyone they were going. There were no cameras or reporters following them around. They just went and volunteered as relief workers.[1]

In September, just two months after Bono played on a bright, worldwide stage, he and Ali slept in a tent for more than a month as they lived in Wello, Ethiopia. Working at a feeding station surrounded by barbed wire, they were in charge of the station's orphanage.

"In the morning," Bono recalled, "as the mist would lift, we would see thousands of people walking in lines toward the camp, people who had been walking for great distances through the night—men, women, children, families who'd lost everything, taking their few remaining possessions on a voyage to meet mercy."[2]

The heartbreak and despair of extreme poverty settled like the mist on their camp. One day a man walked up to Bono and held out a small child in his arms. "You take my son," the man said. "He'll live if you take him." Bono was dumbfounded. That moment, talking with the father of that child, formed Bono's commitment to Africa.

As Bono and Ali were flying home on the plane, they agreed that neither of them would ever forget everything they had experienced in Africa.[3] The faces of children they had known and loved in Ethiopia were embedded in their hearts as deeply as tattoos. "I swore I'd never forget what happened in that month," Bono said later. "You say you'll never forget but you get back to your daily life, you get back to the chores, you get back to your passions, but something stayed with me."[4]

Bono had fallen in love with the people of Africa. And love was making a move.

The following year Bono and Ali visited war-torn Central America. During their trip, they met mothers who had lost their children and villagers who had fled their ruined homes. Instead of going to work on this trip, they went to witness the desperation that confronted relief programs. It didn't take long to see just how extreme the situation was.

One day during the visit, Bono and Ali went to an area controlled by a gang of rebels. They were crossing a road when they saw some soldiers on the other side. Bono noticed that the soldiers looked a little worried.

All of a sudden, there was a popping sound as bullets whipped through the air over Bono's head. Everyone in the group froze, listening to their hearts thumping in their chests. Was it gunfire? Should they stay where they were? Should they run for cover?

The soldiers started laughing at their fright. They were "letting us know that they don't like us and they could take our life if they really wanted to," Bono explained. Everyone was terrified, except the group leader. He didn't show any fear. "They're just trying to scare us," he said. "Keep walking. Not a problem."

Not a problem? thought Bono. *What's a problem? Grenades?*[5]

Just as Bono's trip to Ethiopia helped him understand extreme poverty and human suffering in a new way, his visit to Central America shed light on the complex nature of life in other countries. "Some images just overpower the eye," he said. "They just storm your brain and take prisoner of it. I have so many of those experiences. Sometimes I just don't want to share them … It overpowers you in moments when you are really not expecting to. You find yourself walking down a street with tears rolling down your face. [There are] pictures that you can never be separate from."[6]

Songs from the Sadness

When Bono returned to the studio with U2, he did what came naturally to a writer with a melody: expressed his haunting memories in music. He composed two songs born out of his experiences. The somber melody of "Mothers of the Disappeared" revealed the true plight of women whose children were taken by the government in Central America. For "Bullet the Blue Sky" the loud, dissonant sound was completely different as Bono told Edge to "put El Salvador through his amplifier."[7]

In the middle of recording, more tragedy struck. Bono's assistant and friend Greg Carroll died in a motorcycle collision with a drunk driver. Bono had just arrived in America when he heard the news. "I had been in my hotel one hour after a thirteen-hour flight," he said. "I caught the next plane back to Dublin." [8]

Heartsick, Bono and Larry attended the traditional Maori funeral for Greg in his home country of New Zealand. They dedicated the new album to their lost mate and wrote for him the song "One Tree Hill," named after a volcano in New Zealand.

These three songs along with eight other tracks made up U2's fifth studio album, *The Joshua Tree*. The album rose to the tops of the charts in twenty-two countries. In the United Kingdom, it went platinum in two days,

Bono performs songs from *The Joshua Tree* album with folk singer Bob Dylan during a 1987 Inglewood, California, concert at the Forum.

making it the fastest selling record ever released. In Holland, ninety-two thousand concert tickets sold in less than an hour.[9] It earned great critical reviews, sent four songs to the number-one spot, earned Grammy Awards for Album of the Year and Best Rock Performance, and landed U2 on the cover of *Time* magazine as "Rock's Hottest Ticket." Selling twenty-five million copies, *The Joshua Tree* is still one of the world's all-time bestselling albums. It was so popular that twenty years later,

Bono sings on a Los Angeles rooftop during the filming of the video "Where the Streets Have No Name."

in 2007, U2 rereleased the album for an anniversary edition.

The success of the album shot the band members like human cannonballs on a wild circus ride, including this dizzying three-week stretch: In March, the song "With or Without You" became U2's first number-one single in the U.S. Six days later, while fans (and police) gathered on the street, the band performed a rooftop concert in Los Angeles where they filmed the video for "Where the Streets Have No Name." Three days later Bono fell off the stage in a rehearsal for The Joshua Tree tour, enduring a cut that left a permanent scar. Three days after that, U2 opened their tour, and Bono took the stage with a strained voice and a political statement. A week later they gave a show in Nevada only hours before they took to the twinkling Las Vegas strip to film the video for "Still Haven't Found What I'm Looking For."

Along the tour there were sellouts and stadiums and number-one singles. And there were unfortunate events involving tear gas, spray paint, and a dislocated shoulder (to go with the gash on the chin). For nine months the exhilarating, exhausting circus spun on as U2 performed 109 shows in front of more than three million people.

Their next endeavor was born right out of their circus lives. *Rattle and Hum* began as a small documentary about the band on the road.[10] It showed behind-the-scenes footage of The Joshua Tree tour and followed the band as they explored American music in all its diversity. The corresponding album included elements of blues, folk, and country, in addition to rock 'n' roll. The film showed the band's performances with unique American musicians like New Voices of Freedom Harlem Choir, B. B. King, and Bob Dylan.

Sometime during production the project swelled to include a double album and book — much bigger than the original idea. The film was criticized as self-important for rockers so young on the scene. Bono disagreed, arguing that the band approached the music legends as fans, not equals. But while the film did poorly, the album topped music charts in the United States, the United Kingdom, and Australia. *Rattle and Hum* became one of the biggest albums of 1988.

Bono sings the song "Elevation" during their Elevation Tour 2001 at the Molson Center in Montreal, Quebec, October 12, 2001.

AP Images

The band's last tour of the decade, the Lovetown tour, ended in Dublin, the city where it all began. At midnight on December 31, 1989, U2 opened their final show. They played "Where the Streets Have No Name" as the audience counted down the last seconds of the '80s. Fans throughout Europe listened to the concert live on the radio.

The Joshua Tree had been U2's most successful album to date, and they followed it up with another great album.

Critics and listeners expected the band to continue writing, recording, and performing this same kind of music. But the band wanted to do the unexpected. Bono said, "I felt that the spirit of our band was so strong—the musical spirit—and I wanted to find out what would happen if you cut down the Joshua Tree so to speak."[11] Refusing to look back, they wanted to keep pushing and keep discovering what more they could do.

From the Dublin stage on that New Year's Eve, Bono hinted at the band's intentions. "We've had a lot of fun over the last few months," he said into the mic, "just getting to know some of the music which we didn't know so much about—and still don't know very much about, but it was fun!... This is just the end of something for U2 ... We have to go away and ... dream it all up again."

Chapter 7

Fresh Inspiration and a Side of Revenge

It's in the things I do and say
If I want to live, I've got to die to myself someday

"Surrender"
From *War*

New Vibe

On Bono's twenty-ninth birthday, he received the best gift he could have imagined—his first daughter, Jordan. A strong mix of emotions—pride, love, fear–surged through Bono at once. The greatest rock star in the world had been overwhelmed by a tiny baby. "I just felt this love for this beautiful little girl who was so fragile and so vulnerable," he said.[1]

Bono's dad was as delighted as they were. "He loved kids, loved his grandchildren," Bono explained. "His big thing, of course, was when I would have children, I would find out what it was like to be a father. The pain, the torture, et cetera. So when I went and told him that Ali was pregnant, he burst out laughing. He couldn't stop laughing. I said: 'What are you laughing at?' He said: 'Revenge.'" [2]

In 1991 Bono and Ali welcomed their second daughter, Memphis Eve.

As Bono's family grew, the band discussed ending their partnership. After ten years of nonstop recording and performing, they needed a break from all the concerts and composing. With families and other responsibilities dividing their attention, could they really maintain the intensity of creating another album? More importantly, did they believe they could be not just a great band, but the greatest band?

They did.

Making the next record, which they would eventually title *Achtung Baby*, proved harder than they thought. U2 never followed "recipes for success," playing whatever kind of music was popular or had worked for them in the past. So every record was like starting from scratch. They took strands of ideas, developed each one through painstaking collaboration, and knit together lyrics with rhythms and melodies. Playing off each other's ideas and talents, each member of the band made important contributions to the songs that were being written. The collaboration of four musically talented, fiercely diverse individuals always made for an intense process, even if it was rewarding in the end. "Different points of view makes you better," Bono said. "And the thing that'll make you less and less able to realize your potential is a room that's empty of argument."[3]

As they worked through a palette of ideas for the next album, they argued about design and sound. Hoping to gain inspiration, they started recording in Berlin. Years earlier the city had been divided into two separate halves by a huge, stone wall that was guarded by soldiers. The east side of the city was controlled by the Soviet government who kept strict control of their citizens. In 1989, the wall was dramatically torn down and Berlin became a unified city.

Bono, Edge, Larry, and Adam took the last plane into East Germany before the reunification.[4] Berlin was charged with the excitement of change and hope, and Bono thought that recording in such a place would give them inspiration for their next album. But things did not go according to plan. "I think it's fair to say that Larry and Adam weren't as excited about this particular project as myself and Edge," Bono said later. "And I think it's also fair to say that as usual they were right about the songs, i.e. there weren't any." Grinning, he recounted the types of exchanges between himself and the drummer.

"Larry was saying, 'This is a great idea, but where are the songs?'"

"[But I was enthusiastic.] 'We're in Berlin! We can hang out here!'"

"'I don't want to hang out here. I like hanging out in the cold in my own home. It's winter.'"

" 'But the wall has come down! It's a whole new Germany!' "

" 'I want to put up a wall. In my own garden.' "

Bono's humorous recollection belied the serious tension at the time. The entire band saw their situation declining like the old Hansa studio they sat in. "The cold war was breaking out in our band, just as it was ending [in Germany]," the lead singer remarked.[5]

And then, as Bono said, "God walked through the room."

Improvising at the microphone, U2 played a song that the whole world would come to know as "One." After the long struggle, the melody for this song actually flowed freely and surprisingly easily. "Anything where you bump into something that's bigger than you, I do believe is a gift from God, and God is the Creator so creativity comes from there," Bono said. "And you're trying to struggle to get out of yourself. It's a journey away from self-consciousness."[6]

Indeed "One" has been called one of the greatest songs of all time. "In all honesty," Bono said, "it's a song not just about a relationship that's struggling to stay together. The background of it was a *band* that was struggling to stay together."[7]

"One" proved to be the creative breakthrough the group needed. Encouraged by the progress and an enthusiastic producer, the band's resolve returned. U2 returned to Dublin to complete their seventh studio album, *Achtung Baby* (which means "Attention Baby" in German). Little did they know that this album, which had been such a labor to create, would, in 2010, be voted the most influential record of the past twenty-five years.

Bono discussed the record in an interview. He said, "It's a con, in a way. We call it *Achtung Baby*, grinning up our sleeves in all the photography. But it's probably the heaviest record we've ever made."

Same U2, different packaging. *Achtung Baby* replaced obvious sincerity of *The Joshua Tree* with self-mocking flash. In earlier years they had been criticized for being too serious and self-righteous. Bono and the rest of the band knew that their message was important, but they found a new way to present it.

While the style of *Achtung Baby* was certainly new for the band, their concert tour, called Zoo TV, was an even bigger change. There were huge screens and big effects. The cool technology blended with mass media like it was on a caffeine overload. Video screens blitzed the senses with rapid special effects and pop culture images. Through all this, the band tried to show how the world's culture was affected by technology and the media, greed and selfishness. And they were having fun with it. While Zoo TV's wild style never faded throughout the two-year tour, the show's details did change. Special guests made appearances. Most memorable, however, were Bono's alter egos or characters.

These alter egos were all about changing the delivery of the group's message. When playing these characters, Bono said things the audience knew he would never say, just to get people to wake up and pay attention.

Sometimes Bono dressed up as The Fly. He wore

leather pants and a leather coat, as well as big, dark sunglasses. This character was a stereotypical rock star, strutting around the stage with flashy arrogance. Egotistic and vain, The Fly craved the spotlight because he loved the show, and he loved himself even more.

On other occasions, Bono appeared as Mirror Ball Man. In this costume, he wore a shiny silver suit with matching boots and cowboy hat. Mirror Ball Man was a parody of greedy American televangelists (like the one who had angered Bono in that hotel room during his first trip to New York). Preoccupied with himself and his money, this oily-slick character considered success a sure sign of God's blessing.

Finally, Bono entered the stage dressed as the devil — if the devil was a theatrical, old superstar longing for the good old days. As Mr. MacPhisto Bono preened before the audience, self-satisfied and flamboyant with his gold suit, heavy makeup, and short red horns. This character was funny but dark, his lies tainting everything he said. Sometimes MacPhisto called local politicians from the stage and applauded their questionable decisions. (If you're flattered by the devil, you know something is wrong!) Bono had fun with the character and his mischief was reflected in MacPhisto's sincerity.

Along with the variety of characters, U2 performed a variety of hits, including songs from a new album called *Zooropa*, which released during a break in the tour.

During some special shows they interrupted the light, mocking tone of the concert to broadcast live, unscripted reality: satellite transmissions from war-torn Sarajevo,

Bono contemplates the destruction in the Sarajevo library on December 31, 1995, during a private visit to Sarajevo. Bono, who helped organize concerts in support of Sarajevo during the war, took advantage of peace to visit the city.

a city in Bosnia where different ethnic and religious groups had been at war for years.

By the end of the ever-changing show, Bono had recorded and released U2's Grammy-winning album *Zooropa*, recorded a duet with legend Frank Sinatra, made prank calls to the White House, and started a love affair with a broken city in Bosnia.

Several years later, he partnered with an American journalist who had participated in the Zoo TV Sarajevo satellite broadcasts. Together they created the award-winning documentary *Miss Sarajevo*.

The film focused on life in the capital city of Bosnia during a modern war. For four years, citizens in the city struggled to maintain the appearance of normality while gunfire from snipers exploded across the rooftops, and while they went months without electricity or running water.

In the disquieting theme song of the documentary, Bono merged opera and rock into a lingering melody. In 1995 Bono and Edge performed it with opera legend Luciano Pavarotti in Modena, Italy. Another live performance of "Miss Sarajevo" wouldn't happen again until they sang it inside the war-torn city itself.

Popped

U2 pushed for more creative discovery with their next album, *Pop*. Exploring new technology and sound takes time, however, and the album got hung up in the recording studio. While some deadlines can be delayed, the 1997 tour schedule was not one of them. Tickets to upcoming concerts had already been sold. Dates were set in stone. The show had to go on.

Opening in Las Vegas, Nevada, the PopMart tour poked fun at popular culture and the commercial concept of *Buy! More! Now!* Bono didn't wave white flags on this tour as he had during the concerts for *War*. In quite a different picture—which was sometimes misunderstood and sometimes dismissed—the show's message was ironic, extravagant, and deliberately over-the-top.

Bono and Luciano Pavarotti perform at the Pavarotti and Friends concert on May 27, 2003, in Modena, Italy.

Bono acknowledged that the tour went well every-where but the United States. "And perhaps there's a reason for that," he explained. "We opened in Las Vegas. And we had there this giant drive-in screen, [and] this mirror ball lemon that came out like a spaceship in the middle of the audience. We had this McDonalds M that we were playing under. And *no one noticed*. It was just like every other ride in Las Vegas."[8]

Since the band's recording time went long, it didn't have enough time to rehearse for the live shows. Consequently the music wasn't really where they wanted it to be, and the ambitious, oversized shows suffered a host of technical difficulties. At the end of the concerts, the band began their encores by emerging from the giant, revolving mirror-ball lemon. Unfortunately the lemon spaceship didn't always work the way a proper lemon spaceship should. Twice the band got stuck in the fruit. Bono laughed about it later. "I still miss our lemon," he said. "That was a beautiful psychedelic kind of funky. It was a beautiful thing, traveling in that lemon."

The band spent most of the 1990s deconstructing their serious image but not entirely abandoning it. The music they made still electrified their listeners and affected their hearts. In the middle of the PopMart tour, U2 brought music to war-torn Sarajevo. They were the first band able to host a concert there after the four-year siege. U2 tried to include all ethnic groups in the crowd of fifty thousand. Trains ran for the first time in years, just to bring people to the concert.

It was a bold live performance of big rock stars with soft hearts. Fittingly, they included a special rendition of "Miss Sarajevo" in their set.

Bono later called the Sarajevo show "one of the toughest and one of the sweetest nights of my life." For the city, it was pure love. "For two magical hours," the Associated Press reported, "the rock band U2 achieved what warriors, politicians, and diplomats could not: They united Bosnia."

The Sarajevo show remained an emotional highlight in an otherwise difficult tour. In Los Angeles the crowd sat back and passively watched the show, like taking in a movie. "And music's not like that for us," Bono said. On the other end of the spectrum, the crowd in Sarajevo surged with hopeful energy, as the crowd and the band witnessed the uniting power of music.[9]

Ultimately U2 played ninety-three shows to nearly four million fans. So the tour brought in a lot of money, but it cost even more to produce. U2 actually risked going bankrupt to make the tour happen.

Unsearchable Things

While U2 was in danger of bankruptcy, Bono focused on a different kind of deal. "I think celebrity is ridiculous, but it's currency. We try to spend ours wisely. We try to put it to some use."[10]

This was certainly true when Bono became a spokesman for the Jubilee 2000 campaign. This campaign put him shoulder to shoulder with power brokers, like former U.S. President Bill Clinton and British Prime Minister Tony Blair. Bono argued that the new millennium was the ideal time to forgive the debts of the world's poorest countries so they could afford to care for their own people.

Whenever a country borrows money, it is required to pay back the original amount *plus interest*. For every dollar countries in Africa borrowed, it owed back eight dollars—a backbreaking amount even for a wealthy nation, let alone a poor one. Most of the money African nations received from foreign aid, then, went to pay off loans instead of to support the starving, hurting people who needed the money most.

Bono spoke about it at the National Prayer Breakfast in Washington, DC. "If your brother becomes poor, the

Scriptures say, and cannot maintain himself, you shall maintain him. You shall not lend him your money at interest nor give him your food for profit. This is such an important idea, Jubilee, that this is how Jesus begins his ministry." Jesus ushered in an era of grace, Bono said, and we are still in it. "One thing we can all agree—all faiths, all ideologies—is that God is with the vulnerable and the poor. God is in the slums and the cardboard boxes where the poor plays house. God is in the silence of a mother who has infected her child with a virus that will end both their lives. God is in the cries heard under the rubble of war. God is in the debris of wasted opportunity and lives. And God is with us, if we are with them."[11]

Bono spent much of his time working for the success of Jubilee 2000. In between engagements he flew back to Dublin to join the band in the studio.

With each new album, U2 sought to create fresh music that was original, unique, and relevant. And, as had come to be expected, recording sessions took longer than they planned (in no small part because of Bono's busy schedule). But this time, unlike with *Pop*, U2 refused to be rushed, and they postponed the release of the record. The group stepped back from the extravagance of their earlier experimentation and took away all the glitter from alternative techno sounds. What remained were the strong melodies.

Anxious fans had to wait months before they could hear the band's new music, but when the finished product was released in October 2000, listeners weren't disappointed. *All That You Can't Leave Behind* debuted at number one in twenty-two countries. The single "Beautiful Day"—a song that uplifted a vast Super Bowl audience a year later—won three Grammy Awards.

The album's simple black-and-white cover art reflected the straightforward, sometimes understated sound as well. The photograph on the cover showed the band standing in an airport, as if waiting to depart. A sign directing passengers to the correct gate originally read *F21–36,* but Bono had the photo changed so the sign read *J33–3.* This referred to the Bible verse Jeremiah 33:3 (*Call to me and I will answer you and tell you great and unsearchable things you do not know*). Bono referred to it as God's own phone call. (Jeremiah 33:3 made another appearance on U2's 2009 album *No Line on the Horizon.* The intimate worship song "Unknown Caller" contains the lyric "3:33 when the numbers fell off the clock face.")

Bono and Ali's third child, Elijah Bob Patricius Guggi Q, was born on their seventeenth wedding anniversary, before the album was released. Like a bookend, their fourth child, John Abraham, was born after the release, just as the Elevation tour was getting under way.

Five months later, Bono's dad was admitted to the hospital in the last stages of cancer. Bono went to be with him.

"I got to make peace with him, but never really to become his friend," Bono said. In his last days, Bono visited him every day in the hospital, but all his father could do was whisper.

Bono spent many evenings lying beside Bob Hewson on a roll-up bed. Sometimes he drew pictures of his father's hospital room, complete with all the wires and tubes. And sometimes he would read. Bob loved the rich language of Shakespeare, and Bono read plays to his dad.[12]

After his father died, Bono went onstage in London to continue the European tour and to pay tribute to his dad. "We all want to thank my old man for giving me this voice," Bono said into the mic. "He was a fine tenor, and said to me if only I'd had [his] voice, just think what could [have happened]." Then Bono sang "Kite," a song he had written for his own children. "This is for you, Bob," he said.[13]

The tribute spoke volumes about Bono's love for his father. Even if things were never perfect between them, Bono cherished the memory of his dad. "I suppose I didn't have a great relationship with my father for a long time," Bono said. "I . . . made peace with him before he died, but I wished I had put that right earlier."[14]

All those emotions showed up in the music. Bono's personal tribute to his dad came on the next U2 album, *How to Dismantle an Atomic Bomb.*

"His demise set me off on a journey, a rampage, a desperate hunt to find out who I was," Bono explained, "and that resulted in a lot of these songs."[15]

Specifically "Sometimes You Can't Make It on Your Own" was inspired by Bono's father, the macho Irish opera lover. "In that song there's a note I hit. The line goes, 'I know that we don't talk, but can you hear me when I sing?' And I sing this line and I feel him very strongly. It's hard to sing. And it's hard to even hear it."[16]

The heartfelt tribute went on to win Song of the Year at the 2006 Grammy Awards.

"This is for you, Bob."

Chapter 8

What This Team Needs Is a Pop Star

I would believe if I was able
But I'm waiting on the crumbs from your table

"Crumbs from Your Table"
From *How to Dismantle an Atomic Bomb*

The Crisis and the Emergency

Bono understood the power of working in partnership with others. After all, years in music kept him collaborating with the same band members for decades and also teaming up with diverse talents in opera, R&B, rap, folk, country, and rock. So it was little wonder that he searched out meaningful partnerships in even grander endeavors.

In order to bring mercy to the world in practical, measurable ways, he needed teammates—a lot of them. Bono sang about charity but he understood he could help

Africa even more by calling attention to the continent's plight. "I'm tired of dreaming," he said. "I'm into doing at the moment. It's like, let's only have goals that we can go after. U2 is about the impossible. Politics is the art of the possible. They're very different, and I'm resigned to that now." He still performed in sold-out stadiums, but he also spent his time rallying people to the cause of the poverty stricken.

"Two-and-a-half million Africans are going to die next year for the stupidest of reasons: because it's difficult to get the AIDS drugs to them," Bono said. "Well, it's not difficult to get fizzy drinks to the furthest ... reaches of Africa. We can get cold, fizzy drinks. Surely, we can get the drugs. This is America. We can do anything here. You've got a guy on the moon. You know what I mean?"[1]

Receiving the right medication affects not only whether a child lives but how *well* he lives and how well he *learns*. Health and education are linked. Treat the illness—AIDS or malaria or lice—and schools and learning are no longer mere dreams. "In the not-too-distant future," said Bono, "the rich world will invest in the education of the poor world, because it is our best protection against young minds being twisted by extremist ideologies—or growing up without any ideology at all, which could be worse." Help the extremely poor, give them hope of a future, and peace naturally follows.

"I'm arguing for a demonstration to the world of what we're capable of in the West, with our technology, our innovations, our agriculture, our pharmacology," said

President George W. Bush shakes hands with Bono, right, after Bush spoke at the Inter-American Development Bank, March 14, 2002, in Washington.

Bono. "We've developed this unimaginable prosperity. Let's show the world what we can do with it."[2]

The AIDS emergency wasn't the only thing that had Bono working overtime. Helping impoverished people included forgiving national debts so poor countries could develop their own resources, build roads and schools, get medicine to the sick, and raise up a generation free from the endless cycle of poverty.

Bono understood the force he commanded as an individual. He walked onto a stage and the planet paid attention. He knew how to communicate a message. And he would not back down from a fight.

With his unique and powerful voice, Bono helped mobilize the effort to care for the world's poorest. But he knew it was a mission that couldn't be done alone.

Good Deals

For Africa, Bono had to make new collaborations with talents that had nothing to do with music. After all, partnerships can't be forged only with one's friends. "You don't have to be harmonious on everything—just one thing—to get along with someone," Bono pointed out.[3]

Former U.S. Treasury Secretary Paul O'Neill had a common response to the singer that knocked on his door. "I refused to meet him at first," O'Neill said. "I thought he was just some pop star who wanted to use me." But eventually he agreed to sit down and talk with Bono. They talked for an hour and a half, and the treasury secretary changed his opinion. "He's a serious person. He cares deeply about these issues, and you know what? He knows a lot about them."[4]

Bono also talked to then-President Bill Clinton and others, showing how canceling debt can reduce poverty while increasing goodwill toward America.

At a meeting of the world's most powerful heads of government in 2005 (called the G8 Summit), Bono helped convince industrial nations to forgive over forty billion

AP Images

Former President Bill Clinton speaks with Bono before a dinner in New York in honor of the Frank Foundation Child Assistance International of Washington, D.C.

dollars in African loans. "These countries, instead of paying ... old debts can spend it on ... health, education, and infrastructure," he argued. And the heads of state listened. They promised to give access to medicine to almost ten million impoverished people with HIV.[5]

But Bono didn't stop there. He proceeded to seek out then-President George W. Bush and National Security Adviser Condoleezza Rice. "People openly laughed in my face when I suggested that this administration would distribute antiretroviral drugs to Africans," Bono said.

"They said, 'You are out of your tiny mind.'" But Bono remained persistent, and eventually the administration promised an astonishing gift of five hundred million dollars to help stop the spread of AIDS in Africa. "There [are] two-hundred thousand Africans now who owe their lives to America," Bono said proudly in 2005.[6] (The number would continue to go up.)

In his mission, Bono also toured four African countries with U.S. Treasury Secretary O'Neill. He appealed to Canadian prime ministers, statesmen, and four-star generals.

"If you put your shoulder to the door, it might open," said Bono, "especially if you're representing a greater authority than yourself. Call it love, call it justice, call it whatever you want ... Most will agree that if there is a God, God has a special place for the poor. The poor are where God lives. So these politicians should be nervous, not me."[7]

Bono worked with politicians and world leaders on all sides of different political issues. But once again, Bono wasn't willing to stop there. So he went to the church. He reached into the pews and urged those who listened not to stay quiet and meek in the face of such extreme famine and poverty. "God will not accept that," Bono said. "Mine won't, at least. Will yours?"[8]

Motivated by a higher calling, the church took steps to mobilize its massive organization with medicine and mosquito nets that prevent malaria. But not every Christian group got behind the efforts. Many conservative congregations responded weakly, ignoring the struggles of distant Africans with whom they felt they shared little common ground. Bono was furious.

"I was very angry that conservative Christians were not involved more in the AIDS emergency," Bono said. "I was saying, 'This is the leprosy that we read in the New Testament. Christ hung out with the lepers but you're ignoring the AIDS emergency. How can you?'" This time, the conservative Christians listened. They agreed that they needed to be involved in the AIDS crisis, and they began to fund missions to Africa.[9]

Bono also talked with Oprah Winfrey—and her millions of viewers—explaining what was happening in Africa, and how easy it would be for Americans to help change the world. "For the same price of taking your girlfriend to the movies," he said, "you can change their lives. What a privilege to be in that situation."[10]

The bigger the team to tackle the work, the better. Critics argued that some of Bono's partners didn't really care about Africa; they just wanted to look good or be seen with a rock star. But Bono waved off the argument and focused on the critical mission. "The problem just has to be sorted and we can't do it just with governments alone," he said. "We're fighting a fire. The house is burning down. Let's get the water. You end up beside somebody who lives up the road who you don't really like. Do you really care if he's polishing up his image [by] putting the fire out?"[11]

A world united against poverty. Medicine for every sick person on the planet. Bono acknowledged these were "dizzy dreams." Bono kept dreaming. "What makes you qualified to help a person who has been knocked down in a car accident?" Bono asked. "There's only one qualification necessary: that you happened to be there, and you happened to be able to call the ambulance. That's really how I see my role: as raising the alarm."[12]

Getting Busy

Clearly the participation and support of leaders were critical to the effort against poverty. But this big of a crisis needed foot soldiers as well. After all, it is not enough to sound an alarm if there is no good way for people to help. Information and emotion needed to translate to action. "When people get organized, get busy, things change," said Bono.

In 2002 Bono cofounded DATA which stands for Debt-AIDS-Trade-Africa. This group coordinated efforts across geographical boundaries and political lines to find aid for Africa. In 2007 they joined forces with ONE, another organization Bono helped form in 2004. "ONE harasses politicians of all colors into doing the right thing," Bono explained. Using the motto "the campaign to make poverty history," ONE grew to nearly three million campaigners in seven years.[13]

In 2005 Bono helped start a business to encourage trade in Africa. Run by his wife, Ali, EDUN fashion line grew to include eight factories on the continent by 2011.

In 2006 Bono helped found (RED), a fundraising arm which gets businesses and consumers directly involved. People buy from companies like Nike or Apple who have in turn partnered with (RED) and give a portion of their profits to the cause. This way people could contribute to the cause on even the most casual but necessary level. In 2011, the coordinated effort of (RED) had raised $200 million.[14]

Bono worked tirelessly to rally a variety of partners so that love could change the world. It was a huge mission, but in the end, Bono believed that a better world was possible. "It's always the same attitude that wins the day: faith over fear. On the Africa stuff we can't lose, because we're putting our shoulder to a door God Almighty has already opened."[15]

From the Stage

Since Bono leaped from the stage at the Live Aid concert in 1985, U2 used its shows not just to entertain people for a night but to motivate and mobilize audiences for humanitarian causes as well.

When the band highlighted human rights during Amnesty International's Conspiracy of Hope, the organization's membership in the United States grew by forty-five thousand people.

When they protested a nuclear factory in the United Kingdom in a concert, all proceeds went to Greenpeace. In troubled Northern Ireland, they campaigned for the Good Friday Peace Agreement and invited the two leaders of the Catholic and Protestant communities to join them on stage. "This is about a photograph," Bono explained. "And yet we're going to ask you to shake hands,

Juda Ngwenya/Reuters/Landov

Bono and former South African president Nelson Mandela pose after they met at Mandela's residence in Johannesburg, May 25, 2002.

in public, because they'd never done that before. It was a really great moment."[16]

In 2003, U2 went onstage during the Special Olympics World Summer Games to perform "One" and "Pride (In the Name of Love)." At the end, former South African president Nelson Mandela, a rare champion for unity, joined the band onstage to the ecstatic cheers of the crowd.

Bono also helped organize a series of benefit concerts where in July 2005, U2 performed to spotlight the crises of nations facing the AIDS epidemic.

In 2009, U2 played in Germany to celebrate twenty

years since freedom joined East and West Berlin. Their concert at the Brandenburg Gate commemorated the day in November, 1989, that the wall dividing the city tumbled down. "Happy birthday, Berlin!" Bono called out at the show.

Whether for Africa or Sarajevo, Bono's gifts turned a voice into an appeal and a song into a calling. To communicate with a crowd or to partner with a politician you didn't necessarily need a rock star—but if you wanted to move mountains, it didn't hurt to have this one.

"We always believed that the job of music was to change the world," Bono said. "We always believed that. We were sixteen, we believed that, because it changed *our* world. It changed the size of your bedroom, it expanded it … you could go anywhere you want in your head, change the temperature of the room when an amazing song came on … [You heard other artists and thought,] *Of course we can change the world, and who's going to tell us we can't.*"[17]

Chapter 9

Rock It Like You Mean It

When love comes to town, I'm gonna jump that train
When love comes to town, I'm gonna catch that flame

"When Love Comes to Town"
From *Rattle and Hum*

A Dream

Bono was no stranger to Washington, DC. He had worked with a number of governing leaders including two American presidents. In 2008 he returned to the capital of the United States. This time though, he wasn't part of the political circle; he was part of the band.

Forty-six years earlier, civil rights leader Martin Luther King Jr. attracted vast crowds to the Lincoln Memorial. There he gave his historic speech that inspired a nation. "I have a dream today!" he exclaimed.

Now it was a different decade, and U2 was set up in the exact same place, celebrating the inauguration of the first black U.S. president. As the band started to play, Bono repeated another memorable phrase from King, "Let freedom ring." U2 played, "Pride (In the Name of Love)," and Bono belted the lyrics that specifically referred to King: "Free at last, they took your life. They could not take your pride. In the name of love, what more in the name of love."

The parallels weren't lost on the band. Not only had the musicians written about the American civil rights leader they admired, but they had played video clips of this very speech at past concerts. Now they looked out at the same view King saw for sixteen minutes at a podium.

"It was a very odd thing," Bono said thoughtfully. "The steps of the Lincoln Memorial where we played the song that we wrote when we were twenty-three years old ... these were the steps [where] King made that speech, and now you're seeing this sort of history march on with [President] Obama. It was very odd to be there."[1]

Moving Target

In thirty years the music industry has undergone massive change. Technology, varieties, and venues are totally different. Television and radio are hardly the only outlets. It's hard to conceive that the same band that started three decades ago could not only weather the change, but stay ahead of it and on top. They remained current by speaking to each generation, by riding the waves of change instead of swimming in one place.

MP3 players, iPods, mobile phones, and other digital music devices changed how people listened to their music. And it was increasingly rare for fans to listen to a whole, unified album, with each song building on the last to form a theme.

Coming up with great music was no longer enough. In the new millennium *what* Bono sang or said was just as important as *how* he chose to say it. "We have to start thinking about new ways of getting our songs across," Bono said, "of communicating in this new world with so many channels."[2]

In 2006, a group of filmmakers approached U2. They had an idea about making a concert film that involved state-of-the-art 3D technology. It was a huge project that threatened to distract them from their Vertigo tour. But U2 took the chance to be part of a cutting-edge experiment.

After shooting seven concerts in Latin America and two in Australia, *U23D* was released in 2008. It was the first film shot, produced, and screened entirely in 3D. The eleventh-highest grossing concert film of all time, it holds a spot right below U2's 1988 film *Rattle and Hum.*

Later the band broke new ground on their 2010 concert film as well. Twenty-seven high definition cameras were used to film their show in Pasadena, California. The same concert holds the distinction as the first one ever to be streamed live on YouTube.

Their hit "Vertigo" got some unusual airtime—on

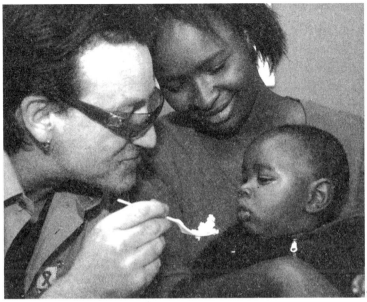

Bono spoon-feeds eleven-month-old Thomas Qubile while his mother, Mpumelelo, looks on at the prenatal HIV clinic of the Chris Hani Baragwanath Hospital in Soweto, South Africa.

a television commercial for iPods. The ad looked more like a music video than a commercial. But some critics accused the band of selling out. They said that the band had diminished their music by using it for commercials. These critics thought that when fans heard the song on the radio, they would associate it with an advertisement instead of what it was really trying to say.

Bono disagreed. "*Selling out* is doing something you don't really want to do for money," he argued. "That's what selling out is. We asked to be in the ad. We could see where rock music is, fighting for relevance next to hip-hop."[3]

Agree with the move or not, a lot of young kids could now sing along with "Vertigo" even if they'd never heard of U2. For a new generation, "Vertigo" was the beginning of a lifelong relationship with the band. "If you pour your life into songs, you want them to be heard," said Bono. "It's a desire to communicate. A deep desire to communicate inspires songwriting."

At the same time, the band was not interested in writing jingles — or anything that resembled them. U2 was once offered twenty-three million dollars for the music rights to one of their biggest, most recognizable anthems: "Where the Streets Have No Name." A car company wanted to make a commercial using the song. "I know from my work in Africa what twenty-three million dollars could buy," Bono said. "It was very hard to walk away from twenty-three million." But the band knew that if a show was ever a little bit off — if the crowd wasn't energized and their music wasn't sounding the way they wanted it to — they could play "Where the Streets Have No Name" and, as Bono said, God would walk through the room. That was the one song they could rely on to change the mood of an audience and bring their hearts back to the music. Bono, Edge, Larry, and Adam agreed that they didn't want people in the audience to turn to each other when they heard the opening riff of the song and say, "Oh, now they're playing the car commercial." The band turned down the offer.[4]

Thirty-year friends Bono, Edge, Larry, and Adam

wanted to stay in the band as long as it meant staying consistent without being stagnant, pushing creative limits but not losing themselves, and arguing but working toward the same goals. Speaking about his partnership with his three extraordinary friends and bandmates, Bono said, "I want to see what can happen with a band if they keep their integrity, keep their commitment to each other, and ... create extraordinary music ... [What if we] actually stayed in contact with the world, were awake, [and] didn't let the money buy [us] off, you know? I'm still hungry. I still want a lot out of the music."[5]

New Heights

After the 2004 album *How to Dismantle an Atomic Bomb*, Bono revealed that once again, U2 would go in a different musical direction. "We're going to continue to be a band, but maybe the rock will have to go; maybe the rock has to get a lot harder. But whatever it is, it's not gonna stay where it is."

The public would wait five years for another studio album.

To start recording U2 settled in an unlikely place — an open courtyard in a hotel in the religious capital of Morocco.

Not only did they experiment musically, but Bono experimented writing songs from another point of view, like that of a police officer or a soldier. "The characters in the songs have been to places I haven't been — at least physically," he explained. "It really freed me up. I was sick of singing about myself ... I could sing from as deep a place by putting myself in different predicaments."[6]

The band recorded four songs in one take. "That took two hours," Bono remarked. "The rest of the album took two years."[7] Ultimately it took three producers, more than fifty song concepts, and studios in four different countries. In February 2009, U2 released their twelfth studio album, *No Line on the Horizon.*

The record turned out to be more "intense" than they expected. "I like music to be joyous," Bono said. "But you're only in charge of a certain amount of what you're doing."[8]

The subsequent tour took the group's live performance to new heights. "We were never really good at being on camera really," Bono said. "But when we were in front of a crowd, magic happened between us and our audience, and the songs even started to make more sense ... To this day that's where we do our best work, and that's where the songs live."[9]

U2 had long outgrown cozy clubs, but the band still pursued close connections with their audience, no matter how big the crowd. So Bono liked to perform totally surrounded by the fans. But this wasn't as simple to pull off as it sounded. A band can perform "in the round" in an indoor arena because lights, speakers, and equipment can hang from the ceiling. But even the best band can't hang gear from the sky in an open stadium.

"Our idea was really to have the audience be on stage there with you," Bono explained. "We were trying to find a way to do that outdoors." Edge remembered Bono using forks to make a primitive version of his vision.

"[I] kind of built how it might possibly work," Bono recalled, "but just as a sort of—as an idiot, not understanding the engineering implications." The idea (and Bono's silverware construction) was the first tiny step of an enormous undertaking.[10]

Creative teams and technical engineers were brought together to make possibilities into realities. The stage had to be big enough to support heavy equipment, but it also had to be transported. "Think about a rock show like 360 as the same scale as a gigantic action film, except you're moving location every few days," Bono explained. "You're building a whole town, a whole city, and then you're knocking it down, putting it into trucks and then moving it the next day."[11]

Concepts were sketched out, altered, refined, and perfected. It took a year to construct the first stage and required 165 trucks and three sets of steel.[12] At the center of the structure was a mammoth, moving, cone-shaped screen that in itself proved to be an expensive engineering puzzle. Completely original, it had to be conceived, calculated, and constructed from every large panel to the last little pixel.[13]

Finally everything came together, and on June 30, 2009, U2 unveiled the gigantic centerpiece of the U2 360 tour. Nicknamed "The Claw," the structure combined art and science, intimate and massive. U2 performed the inaugural show in Barcelona, Spain, under The Claw, in the middle of their fans. Later the concert in the Rose

AP Images

U2 performs during their 360 tour at Wembley Stadium in London, Friday, August 14, 2009.

Bowl Stadium in Pasadena, California, set the record for the highest attendance for a United States show by one headliner. (The previous record holder was also U2, set in 1987.)[14]

The circular screen provided close-ups of the band and took the audience outside the stadium, sometimes *way* outside the stadium. South African Archbishop Desmond Tutu and Burmese Nobel Peace Prize winner Aung San Suu Kyi delivered individual, personal statements. From an even farther corner of the universe, Belgium's astronaut Commander Frank De Winne drifted on screen. Filmed at the International Space Station in outer space, he looked into a camera to face as many as a hundred thousand fans. Floating without gravity, he spoke the lyrics from U2's "In a Little While": "Man dreams one day to fly," he said softly. "A man takes a rocket ship into the skies. He lives on a star that's dying in the night and follows in the trail the scatter of light."

Bono was moved. "It's one thing out of my mouth. Hearing [it] out of his mouth, that's a very touching moment."[15]

The tour was groundbreaking and successful. "Got to try and give them at the very least something they've never seen before or maybe more importantly something they haven't felt before," said Bono. "Because in the end, for all this architecture and sci-fi stuff, if you don't feel the songs and the band, what is the point?"[16]

Chapter 10

Rise Up and Rock

And there's heat in the sun to see us through the rain
Do you feel loved

"Do You Feel Loved"
From *Pop*

Small Change for Big Change

In the New Testament, Jesus modeled to his disciples how to pray. "Our Father in heaven, hallowed be your name, your kingdom come, your will be done, on earth as it is in heaven" (Matthew 6:9–10). Jesus continued the personal appeal that communicated praise and trust in God. For Bono the Lord's Prayer was also a call to action.

Your kingdom come on earth. "Our purpose is to bring heaven to earth in the [small] as well as the [larger picture]," he explained. "In every detail of our lives we

94

should be trying to bring heaven to earth. Have the peace that passes understanding [Philippians 4:7] at the center of yourself, but do not be at peace with the world because the world is not a happy place for most people who are living in it. And the world is more malleable than you think. And we can wrestle it from fools."[1]

Bono continued to wrestle.

On May 5, 2010, Bono went with Ali and Adam to a movie premiere in New York. Not a Hollywood blockbuster, this movie was produced by (RED) about Africa to help Africa. Entitled "The Lazarus Effect," the title referred to the New Testament miracle when Jesus brought Lazarus back from the dead. The documentary followed the stories of sick people who, with access to medicine, came back from the edge of death themselves.

In Zambia one out of seven people are infected with incurable HIV.[2] "For every person you treat, two more are infected and you get pandemics," explained Bono.[3]

With antiretroviral drugs, AIDS can be treated, and the hopeless find hope. *The Lazarus Effect* considered the Zambian doctors and some of their patients who got treated, got strong, got inspired to help their country grow healthy.

At the movie premiere, Bono proclaimed the profound results of the medicine. "How simple it is," he said, "to have an impact on a life that's vulnerable, whether that's a child, a mother, whether it's a man who wants to be part of the workforce but is now half his body weight begging for his life. Two pills a day—forty days later he's back at work."[4]

The daily dose of this medicine costs forty cents. An amount that an American might find in his couch cushions proves very expensive to a sick person halfway around the world. Bono sees it as a grand opportunity. "When you realize how simple it is to change the course of someone's life, somebody who has got HIV AIDS ... you get excited about being part of the solution." [5]

Tour Interrupted

Five days after *The Lazarus Effect* premiere, Bono was preparing for the North American leg of the 360 tour, anticipating headlining the Glastonbury Festival, and celebrating his and his daughter's shared birthday. He didn't feel great but pressed on through his busy schedule. "I was trying to pretend there was something not wrong," Bono recalled with a smile. "And then Edge pointed out that I wasn't able to walk and that I was on a cane and that I was lying down during lunch." [6]

The problem couldn't be ignored any longer. The day after his birthday, Bono got an MRI and met with a German physician. "Have you lost the use of your left leg?" the doctor asked.

"Actually, yes, I have," Bono replied nonchalantly.

"Are you losing the use of your right leg?" the doctor asked.

The singer looked down at his leg as if for the first time and said, "Actually that just started happening now!"

The doctor got very serious. "Do not move," he said.

"You are in grave danger. We will operate tomorrow morning in Munich in the public hospital."[7]

Pieces of a disc in Bono's spine had broken off and gone down his spinal canal, severing nerves. Without surgical repair, Bono's back would have only gotten worse, the damage eventually becoming life-changing and permanent. In surgery the doctor was able to take care of the injury, but Bono's recovery required complete bed rest. The rock star was laid up for six long weeks.

While Bono followed doctor's orders, there was no other choice but to reschedule appearances and postpone U.S. and Canadian tour dates (some shows for more than a year). Edge joked that it was the first real rest the singer had had in decades.[8]

In the middle of July, Larry got behind a video camera and filmed Bono seated on a chair in a room filled with instruments and sound equipment. A smile on his face, Bono bragged about little things, like sitting and standing. "I am ready, rebuilt by German engineering, better design I'm told," he said into the camera. "It was not a lot of fun for me, but staring at the ceiling has some advantages. Got some great songs which we've been recording."[9]

On August 6, 2010, "The Claw" was set up in Turin, Italy, and U2 returned to the 360 stage. Bono had been here before, but this time it was different. "I was very nervous—very, very nervous," he admitted.[10]

A powerful sense of gratitude filled the stadium—gratitude not just from fans who waited to see a postponed show, but from a worldwide audience, close friends, and loyal crew who were sick of the silence. "Well, when I see Larry Mullen give me a standing ovation, I know something's going on," Bono laughed. "So it was a big night actually, just getting through it."[11]

Two years after the tour opened, eleven months after Bono's return, U2 played the last show of the 360 tour. In the course of a hundred and ten concerts, seven million people in thirty countries saw the band live. "I do things on my own and people always give me great reception wherever I go," Bono said. "It's not the same as walking out on stage with U2. It's an amazing feeling. When the four of us walk out on stage, everyone in the building, their hair stands up on end. I don't know why. Maybe it's something to do [with us] sticking together. Because whether it's a marriage, a relationship, business relationship, mates, family, nobody sticks together. It seems the whole thing in this world is to pull relationships apart." He raised his eyebrows and set his jaw. "Not happening [with this band]." [12]

The Unknown

After such a creative, huge tour, U2 could have stayed very busy playing the same songs to the same large audiences. For Bono that was as excruciating as back surgery. "I'm just not interested in what we've done," he said. "I'm always more interested in what we're about to do."[13]

His next creative venture occurred to him unexpectedly one night at a songwriting award ceremony. Bono and Edge were in the diverse audience next to other accomplished songwriters. During the evening, renowned composer Andrew Lloyd Webber took to the stage. A veteran of musical theater, he had a long list of Broadway productions to his credit. After Webber accepted an award, he gave a speech and thanked many people — including all the "rock people" for not bothering him.

Bono looked at Edge with a mischievous smile. Edge looked at Bono. And at that moment they decided Broadway was in need of some rock people.[14]

It couldn't be more of a challenge. Music and lyrics on Broadway are completely different than music and lyrics on stage at a rock concert. In theater the songs drive a story forward, accompany action, play to a dissimilar audience with particular expectations. It was just the kind of ambitious creative experiment that Bono loved.

So Bono and Edge jumped out of the rock 'n' roll box and into musical theater. They got involved in a concept taken from the comics: *Spider-Man: Turn Off the Dark*. They considered the story, the action, the audience, and the director's vision. They wrote dance songs, campy numbers, and big show tunes. They coordinated horns with strings, solos, and duets.

Their involvement brought a lot of attention and buzz — for good and for bad. The media reported about the aerial stunts, technical innovation, and elaborate production. And it reported the injuries, delays, creative differences, and growing cost. Broadway was used to this process, but it didn't always have the press that rock stars generated. "We come from out of town," Bono smiled, poking fun that he and Edge knew their way around a stage, but not one on Broadway. "We don't expect it to be easy."[15]

In the summer of 2011, after nearly a decade of development, *Spider-Man* finally opened. It was the most expensive, most "technically complex" production to date. In January 2012 it had the highest income for a single week of any show in the history of Broadway.[16]

Chapter 11

The Legacy of the Unelectable

We're one but we're not the same
We get to carry each other, carry each other

> "One"
> From *Achtung Baby*

Light in the Tunnel

In 2011 the ONE foundation recognized amazing improvement in the African AIDS crisis. After years of concentrated effort, significant progress could be measured. By getting treated early, keeping up the treatment, and making sure pregnant women got treated, the epidemic was taking a beating. The ONE campaign saw the light at the end of the tunnel.[1]

"Five million lives have been saved in eight years," Bono said. "It was an unusual combination of people

John Paul Filo/CBS via Getty Images

The Edge and Bono go on the *Letterman Show* to promote their new Broadway show, *Spider-Man*.

on the left and the right [who] got together in the ONE organization (because it's the *one* thing they can agree with)."[2]

As the situation in Africa improved, the nature of aid changed as well. For years the continent needed the charity of a wealthy nation. Now that it had gotten a hand up, it could go forward with alliances, learning from others how to become independent. Bono explained it in 2012, "What's key is that the President of the United States [and other countries are] supporting *African* ideas on how to fix their problem. They're country-owned, country-devised plans in thirty African countries. It's partnership—horizontal relationships not vertical ones."[3]

It was a similar idea with EDUN, the clothing company that Ali led. EDUN invested in Africa by building a transparent business where Africans earned money for goods they produced. Other companies could invest in Africa similarly by developing opportunities in industries like farming. "There are whole new approaches to increase productivity in agriculture," Bono explained, which in itself could conceivably bring fifty million people out of poverty in the next decade.[4]

It's a global effort for a shrinking world. In 2012 Bono met with leaders of twelve key countries—France, Germany, Brazil and more—to encourage cooperation in the effort.[5] He was essentially rallying the world. He'd witnessed the difference it could make, held the children it could rescue, talked to the fathers it could change. He wasn't going to stop now.

A Great Future

In the midst of all the work to be done in his humanitarian efforts, Bono still loved the stage, playing with the guys, and giving expression to the melodies in his head. "Over the years, you ... take for granted the opportunity to make music," he said. "I'm very happy as an activist, but it's a very demanding life, a slog, and it can be dirty work. *[New Line on the Horizon]* put me back in the place I was as a teenager, working in a gas station, dreaming of getting to rehearsal with the band. It was so intoxicating to hear an electric guitar or the silver sound of a cymbal. Maybe I needed to be reminded of that."[6]

He loved creating music, but that didn't mean it came easy. So when he was asked how a great song happened, he couldn't help but joke, "You just wake up and it's finished. It just comes in dreams."[7]

After decades of making music, he knew the exact opposite was true. "You've got to dig a deep well and see what you can pull up."[8]

As always it required an intense process of collaboration between great, lifelong friends who were as different as a guitar and a keyboard. As always Bono valued the conflict as much as the shared history. "As I look around," he explained, "and see people getting older and ridding the room of argument, so they're just left with a small group of friends and family who agree with them, I feel sorry for them. Because friction makes you sharper. Keeps you more awake. Stops the rot of thinking that everything you do is great." And then he smiled adding, "Though in our case it obviously is."[9]

Rumor has it U2 will release its thirteenth studio album in 2013. "There won't be a U2 album unless there's something really special," Bono promised.[10] As a band they keep pursuing greatness. "It's almost impossible to do anything that's great. Turns out that 'very good' can be the enemy of 'great.' Because you get very good just by being around. That's not enough."[11]

Passionate argument to create something great, Bono wouldn't have it any other way. "Edge is in denial of his genius," Bono smiled. "I'm a little too sure of my own. Larry is suspicious of both, and Adam sees merit in both ... As a band there's no sense of entitlement. I think they're very aware that U2's got to do something very special to have a reason to exist right now, so that's what we're doing. They're amazing men. They really are extraordinary. They really, really want it."[12]

What Is Possible

The accomplishments of an Irish musician and his three bandmates are testimony to what can happen when people seek to do the extraordinary. "Don't get too interested in what's possible," Bono said. "The impossible is made possible by a combination of faith, gift, and strategy."[13]

In their long and continuing career, U2 has won more Grammys than any other artist (with last count at twenty-two), including Best Rock Group, Best Rock Album, Album of the Year, Record of the Year, and Song of the Year. In 2005 they were inducted into the Rock and Roll Hall of Fame. Their work has lingered on top-ten charts all over the world, and has won a truckload of international awards. And they've sold enough albums to give a copy to each person in Ireland — and then do it again more than *twenty-six times.*

Bono's list of personal honors runs as long as a U2 hit list. He has been nominated for the Nobel Peace Prize three different times. He has been named a Knight of the Legion of Honour in France, granted honorary knighthood in the United Kingdom, named *Time* magazine's

Bono claps palms with Maasai children during his visit to the traditional Shambasha village near Arusha, Tanzania, during a six-nation tour of Africa.

Person of the Year in 2005, and given the Nobel "Man of Peace" Prize in 2008. Two years later he was awarded the Humanitarian Leadership Award for his work with the ONE Campaign, which continues to rally resources and awareness to fight disease and poverty in Africa. In many ways, this is Bono's life work. "On so many issues it's difficult to know what God wants from us," Bono said, "but on this issue, helping the desperately poor, we know God will bless it."[14]

And the blessings are being felt like ripples across an ocean. "As a result of debt cancellation, there are an extra 40 million children going to school on the continent of Africa," Bono stated.[15] And strides in healthcare that were seemingly impossible have been made. "There was a time when no Africans could afford those little drugs—two pills a day is all it takes to keep you alive, and people are dying—5,000 a day.[16] America has now 5 million people being kept alive by these drugs."[17]

Bono is a man on a mission in a band on a mission. And the other band members are glad that he's still making music. "The good news from our point of view is that he prefers working on music more than anything else," says Edge. "And also he's unelectable."[18]

As a man who has sought to reconcile tragedy and love, stardom and compassion, this son of a Dublin postal worker has followed faith and music in a continuing thread. The music courses through Bono's veins and runs through his heart. So does the haunting memory of a man carrying his son in Ethiopia—*If you take him, he will live.*

Just as U2's music has become bigger than the four men who make it, Bono's work in Africa and other impoverished nations is bigger than any one man. "What I'm hoping," he says, "is that the social movement that is growing around our issues will be so strong that in the event of somebody like me not being around, they won't notice. In the end, social movements carry the day, not rock stars."[19]

Until then, there's Bono.

Endnotes

Chapter 1: When Love Storms a Stadium

1. Tyrangiel, Josh. "Bono's Mission." Posted February 23, 2002. *TIME Magazine Online. www.time.com.*

2. Ibid.

3. Eckstrom, Kevin. "Bono, After Years of Skepticism, Finds Partner in Religion." Posted February 3, 2006. *Religion News Service. www.atu2.com.*

4. Tyrangiel, Josh. "Bono's Mission." Posted February 23, 2002. *TIME Magazine Online. www.time.com.*

Chapter 2: Steinvic von Huyseman Takes on the Tears

1. Wenner, Jann S. "Bono: The Rolling Stone Interview." *Rolling Stone Magazine* 986 (November 3, 2005).

2. Bono. Interview by Larry King. *Larry King Weekend.* CNN, December 1, 2002.

3. Bono. Interview by Vicki Mabrey. *60 Minutes II*, CBS, 2001.

4. Assayas, Michka. *Bono: In Conversation with Michka Assayas.* New York: Berkley Publishing Group (2006), 124.

5. Fry, Maddy. "Bono Biography." *www.atu2.com.*

6. Bono. Interview by Larry King. *Larry King Weekend.* CNN, December 1, 2002.

7. Assayas, Michka. *Bono: In Conversation with Michka Assayas.* New York: Berkley Publishing Group (2006), 14.

8. Wenner, Jann S. "Bono: The Rolling Stone Interview." *Rolling Stone Magazine* 986 (November 3, 2005).

9. Assayas, Michka. *Bono: In Conversation with Michka Assayas.* New York: Berkley Publishing Group (2006), 18.

10. Fry, Maddy. "Bono Biography." *www.atu2.com.*

11. Assayas, Michka. *Bono: In Conversation with Michka Assayas.* New York: Berkley Publishing Group (2006), 13.

12. Bono. Interview by Larry King. *Larry King Weekend.* CNN, December 1, 2002.

13. Wenner, Jann S. "Bono: The Rolling Stone Interview." *Rolling Stone Magazine* 986 (November 3, 2005).

14. Assayas, Michka. *Bono: In Conversation with Michka Assayas.* New York: Berkley Publishing Group (2006), 22–23.

15. Ibid., 271.

16. Wenner, Jann S. "Bono: The Rolling Stone Interview." *Rolling Stone Magazine* 986 (November 3, 2005).

17. Ibid.

Chapter 3: The Drum Kit Saves the Boy

1. Ibid.

2. Assayas, Michka. *Bono: In Conversation with Michka Assayas.* New York: Berkley Publishing Group (2006), 56.

3. Wenner, Jann S. "Bono: The Rolling Stone Interview." *Rolling Stone Magazine* 986 (November 3, 2005).

4. Ibid.

5. Ibid.

6. Assayas, Michka. *Bono: In Conversation with Michka Assayas.* New York: Berkley Publishing Group (2006), 55–56.

7. "Bono and Larry Interview (Part 1/4)." Uploaded April 4, 2007. *www.youtube.com.*

8. Bono. Interview by Dave Stewart. *Off the Record.* HBO, 2006.

9. Bono. Interview by Vicki Mabrey. *60 Minutes II*, CBS, 2001.

10. Assayas, Michka. *Bono: In Conversation with Michka Assayas.* New York: Berkley Publishing Group (2006), 13.

11. Ibid., 57.

12. Ibid.

13. Bono. Interview by Dave Stewart. *Off the Record*. HBO, 2006.

14. Ibid.

15. Assayas, Michka. *Bono: In Conversation with Michka Assayas*. New York: Berkley Publishing Group (2006), 132.

16. Ibid.

17. DeCurtis, Anthony. "The Rolling Stone Interview: Bono." *Rolling Stone Magazine,* October 30, 2007.

18. Assayas, Michka. *Bono: In Conversation with Michka Assayas*. New York: Berkley Publishing Group (2006), 69–70.

19. Bono. Interview by Dave Stewart. *Off the Record*. HBO, 2006.

20. Bono. Interview by Larry King. *Larry King Weekend*. CNN, December 1, 2002.

21. Ibid.

22. Assayas, Michka. *Bono: In Conversation with Michka Assayas*. New York: Berkley Publishing Group (2006), 131.

Chapter 4: The Back Door to Heaven

1. Interview with Bono, August 20, 1983. *www.youtube.com.*

2. Wenner, Jann S. "Bono: The Rolling Stone Interview." *Rolling Stone Magazine* 986 (November 3, 2005).

3. O'Connor, Brendan. "U2: Access All Areas." Posted June 21, 2009. *The Independent. www.independent.ie.*

4. Wenner, Jann S. "Bono: The Rolling Stone Interview." *Rolling Stone Magazine* 986 (November 3, 2005).

5. Assayas, Michka. *Bono: In Conversation with Michka Assayas*. New York: Berkley Publishing Group (2006), 162.

6. Ibid., 163.

7. Ibid., 162–163.

8. Ibid., 163.

9. Bono. *Legends: U2*. VH1, 1998.

10. Assayas, Michka. *Bono: In Conversation with Michka Assayas*. New York: Berkley Publishing Group (2006), 226–227.

Chapter 5: Limo Ride to the Circus

1. Bono. Interview by John Kasich. *Heartland with John Kasich.* Fox News, March 26, 2007.

2. Assayas, Michka. *Bono: In Conversation with Michka Assayas.* New York: Berkley Publishing Group (2006), 183.

3. Ibid., 186.

4. Ibid.

5. "U2 Lyrics Returned After 23 Years." Posted October 22, 2004. *BBC News. www.bbc.co.uk.*

6. Assayas, Michka. *Bono: In Conversation with Michka Assayas.* New York: Berkley Publishing Group (2006), 178.

7. "Interview with Bono, August 20, 1983." *www.youtube.com.*

8. Assayas, Michka. *Bono: In Conversation with Michka Assayas.* New York: Berkley Publishing Group (2006), 232.

9. Attributed to Steve Peake on http://en.wikipedia.org/wiki/Timeline of U2.

10. Bono. *Legends: U2.* VH1, 1998.

11. Assayas, Michka. *Bono: In Conversation with Michka Assayas.* New York: Berkley Publishing Group (2006), 233.

Chapter 6: Memories Tattooed on the Heart

1. Ibid., 248.

2. Ibid., 247.

3. "Oprah Talks to Bono." Posted April 15, 2004. *O Magazine Online. www.oprah.com.*

4. Bono. Interview by John Kasich. *Heartland with John Kasich.* Fox News, March 26, 2007.

5. Assayas, Michka. *Bono: In Conversation with Michka Assayas.* New York: Berkley Publishing Group (2006), 201–202.

6. Ibid., 210–211.

7. Bono. *Legends: U2.* VH1, 1998.

8. Joseph, Carolus. "Irish Band U2 Come to Tangi (Funeral)."

Posted February 5, 2009. *NZ Rock 'n' Roll History Online. www. kiwirock.co.nz.*

9. Bono. *Legends: U2.* VH1, 1998.

10. Ibid.

11. Bono. Interview by Dave Stewart. *Off the Record.* HBO, 2006.

Chapter 7: Fresh Inspiration and a Side of Revenge

1. Assayas, Michka. *Bono: In Conversation with Michka Assayas.* New York: Berkley Publishing Group (2006), 148.

2. Ibid., 25.

3. Ibid., 169.

4. Bono. *Legends: U2.* VH1, 1998.

5. Bono. Interview by Dave Stewart. *Off the Record.* HBO, 2006.

6. Ibid.

7. Ibid.

8. "U2-Bono and Larry About Popmart." 2001. *www.youtube.com.*

9. Ibid.

10. "U2 Uncovered." Interview by Cat Deely. ITV2, 2005. *www.youtube.com.*

11. Remarks at National Prayer Breakfast, February 2, 2006. "U2 Worship," uploaded June 18, 2011. *www.youtube.com.*

12. Assayas, Michka. *Bono: In Conversation with Michka Assayas.* New York: Berkley Publishing Group (2006), 11.

13. "Bono Pays Tribute to Dad at U2 Concert." Posted August 22, 2001. *ABC News Online. www.abcnews.go.com.*

14. Bono. Interview by Larry King. *Larry King Weekend.* CNN, December 1, 2002.

15. "U2: How to Dismantle an Atomic Bomb and Other Success Stories." December 2004. *The Record Music Magazine. www.therecordmag.com.*

16. "U2 Dismantled." Interview by Hannah Sung. MuchMusic, Uploaded April 6, 2009. *www.youtube.com.*

Chapter 8: What This Team Needs Is a Pop Star

1. Bono. Interview by Larry King. *Larry King Weekend.* CNN, December 1, 2002.

2. "The Rolling Stone Interview: Bono." *Rolling Stone Magazine,* October 30, 2007.

3. Assayas, Michka. *Bono: In Conversation with Michka Assayas.* New York: Berkley Publishing Group (2006), 104.

4. Tyrangiel, Josh. "Bono's Mission." Posted February 23, 2002. *TIME Magazine Online. www.time.com.*

5. Bono. Interview by Ed Bradley. *60 Minutes,* CBS, 2005.

6. Ibid.

7. Assayas, Michka. *Bono: In Conversation with Michka Assayas.* New York: Berkley Publishing Group (2006), 137–138.

8. Eckstrom, Kevin. "Bono, After Years of Skepticism, Finds Partner in Religion." Posted February 3, 2006. *Religion News Service. www.atu2.com.*

9. Bono. Interview by Ed Bradley. *60 Minutes,* CBS, 2005.

10. Bono. Interview by Oprah Winfrey. *The Oprah Winfrey Show.* CBS, September 20, 2002.

11. Dakss, Brian. "Bono Seeing 'Red' Over AIDS." Posted January 26, 2006. *The Early Show Online. www.cbsnews.com.*

12. Assayas, Michka. *Bono: In Conversation with Michka Assayas.* New York: Berkley Publishing Group (2006), 165.

13. Bono. Interview by Jon Stewart. *The Daily Show,* November 30, 2011.

14. Ibid.

15. Assayas, Michka. *Bono: In Conversation with Michka Assayas.* New York: Berkley Publishing Group (2006), 105.

16. Interview by Jo Whiley. "Complete MSN Chat, 04.11.02," U2.com and MSN, 2002. *http://u2_interviews.tripod.com/id112.html.*

17. Bono. Interview by Dave Stewart. *Off the Record.* HBO, 2006.

Chapter 9: Rock It Like You Mean It

1. Bono, Interview by Zane Lowe, BBC, March 2009. *www.youtube.com.*

2. Bono. Interview by Greg Kot. "Transcript of Bono Interview." *Chicago Tribune,* May 13, 2005.

3. Ibid.

4. Ibid.

5. Bono. Interview by Ed Bradley. *60 Minutes,* CBS, 2005.

6. Bono, Interview by Zane Lowe, BBC, March 2009. *www.youtube.com.*

7. Bono, Interview by Zane Lowe, BBC, March 2009. *www.youtube.com.*

8. Fricke, David. "Bono Storms Back." Posted August 19, 2010. *Rolling Stone Magazine, www.rollingstone.com.*

9. Bono. Interview by Jonathan Ross. *Friday Night With Jonathan Ross,* BBC. July 17, 2009.

10. *Squaring the Circle: Creating U2360.* 2010. *www.youtube.com.*

11. Ibid.

12. Bono. Interview by Jonathan Ross. *Friday Night With Jonathan Ross,* BBC. July 17, 2009.

13. *Squaring the Circle: Creating U2360.* 2010. *www.youtube.com.*

14. http://en.wikipedia.org/wiki/Timeline of U2.

15. *Squaring the Circle: Creating U2360.* 2010. *www.youtube.com.*

16. Ibid.

Chapter 10: Rise Up and Rock

1. Bono, Interview, "BONO 2012." Uploaded January 21, 2012. *www.youtube.com.*

2. http://en.wikipedia.org/wiki/The Lazarus Effect.

3. Bono. Interview by Jon Stewart. *The Daily Show,* November 30, 2011.

4. Bono. Interview, "U2 frontman Bono lends his rock star status." BBC. May 5, 2010.

5. Bono, Interview, "Lazarus Red Carpet Bono." Uploaded May 4, 2010. *www.youtube.com.*

6. Bono and The Edge. Interview by David Letterman. *Late Show with David Letterman*, CBS, July 2011.

7. Ibid.

8. The Edge, "Word from The Edge on Bono's Injury, 360 Tour & New Songs." May 25, 2010. Uploaded May 25, 2010. *www.youtube.com.*

9. "We're Coming Back." Uploaded July 13, 2010. *www.youtube.com.*

10. Fricke, David. "Bono Storms Back." Posted August 19, 2010. *Rolling Stone Magazine, www.rollingstone.com.*

11. Ibid.

12. "U2 Dismantled." Interview by Hannah Sung. MuchMusic, Uploaded April 6, 2009. *www.youtube.com.*

13. Kirby, Iona. "'Til Death Do Them Part," September 9, 2011. *www.dailymail.co.uk.*

14. Bono. Interview by Jonathan Ross. *Friday Night With Jonathan Ross*, BBC. July 17, 2009.

15. Bono and The Edge. Interview by David Letterman. *Late Show with David Letterman*, CBS, July 2011.

16. http://en.wikipedia.org/wiki/Spider-Man: Turn Off the Dark.

Chapter 11: The Legacy of the Unelectable

1. Bono. Interview by Jon Stewart. *The Daily Show*, November 30, 2011.

2. Bono and The Edge. Interview by David Letterman. *Late Show with David Letterman*, CBS, July 2011.

3. Bono. Interview by Andrea Mitchell. *Andrea Mitchell Reports*. MSNBC, May 2012.

4. Ibid.

5. Ibid.

6. Gundersen, Edna. "'Horizon' Evolves with U2's Audacity, Creativity, Innovation." Posted March 1, 2009. *USA Today Online. www.usatoday.com.*

7. Bono and The Edge. Interview by David Letterman. *Late Show with David Letterman,* CBS, July 2011.

8. http://*www.atu2.com/newalbum/.*

9. "U2 Dismantled." Interview by Hannah Sung. MuchMusic, Uploaded April 6, 2009. *www.youtube.com.*

10. http://*www.atu2.com/newalbum/.*

11. "U2 Dismantled." Interview by Hannah Sung. MuchMusic, Uploaded April 6, 2009. *www.youtube.com.*

12. http://*www.atu2.com/newalbum/.*

13. DeCurtis, Anthony. "The Rolling Stone Interview: Bono." *Rolling Stone Magazine,* October 30, 2007.

14. Tyrangiel, Josh. "The Constant Charmer." Posted December 19, 2005. *TIME Magazine Online. www.time.com.*

15. Bono. "Who Let the Peacenik In?" (Speech given at the Atlantic Council, Washington, DC, April 29, 2010). *www.u2.com.*

16. Interview with Bono in Fez, Morocco (part 3). Posted on March 25, 2009. *www.youtube.com.*

17. Bono. Interview by Jon Stewart. *The Daily Show,* November 30, 2011.

18. Tyrangiel, Josh. "The Constant Charmer." Posted December 19, 2005. *TIME Magazine Online. www.time.com.*

19. DeCurtis, Anthony. "The Rolling Stone Interview: Bono." *Rolling Stone Magazine,* October 30, 2007.

Defender of Faith: The Mike Fisher Story

Kim Washburn

Mike Fisher knows the true meaning of a power play.

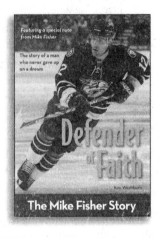

As a veteran of the National Hockey League, Mike Fisher has a lot to be proud of. He plays for the Nashville Predators, was an alternate captain for the Ottawa Senators, competed in the Stanley Cup finals, and has been nominated for the Selke Trophy as the best defensive forward in the league. But it's not just his guts, grit, and talent that have brought him success. His power comes from the top—he puts his faith in Christ first and has demonstrated his love for God both on and off the ice.

Available in stores and online!

Heart of a Champion: The Dominique Dawes Story

Kim Washburn

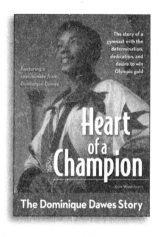

Her determination, dedication, and desire brought home the gold. Dominique Dawes focused on her dream, and nothing would stop her from reaching it—definitely not the fact that she was still just a kid. By the time she was fifteen years old, she stood on the podium to receive the Olympic gold medal in gymnastics. Discover how her faith in God and hard work led her to become one of the top gymnasts in the world. Let her story and her motto of "determination, dedication, and desire" encourage you to become all you can be, in competition and in life. Includes a special note from Dominique Dawes.

Available in stores and online!

Reaching New Heights: The Kelly Clark Story

Natalie Davis Miller

Snowboarder and Olympic Gold Medalist Kelly Clark had accomplished her life's goals by the age of eighteen.

Yet, success didn't leave her feeling fulfilled. Two years later, at an event in Salt Lake City, Kelly stood at the bottom of the pipe, listening to one snowboarder console another who had just crashed: "It's alright. God still loves you." These words led Kelly on a new journey from an Olympian snowboarder into an awesome relationship with Jesus. This story of one of the world's greatest snowboarders will encourage readers young and old to reach for the next level, knowing that God will be with them, win or lose.

Available in stores and online!

Speed to Glory: The Cullen Jones Story

Natalie Davis Miller

He conquered the thing that nearly took his life. At five years old, Cullen Jones nearly drowned. While some people might stay away from water after that, Jones conquered his fear when his mother enrolled him in a swimming class. Not only did he learn to swim, he quickly found that he was a good swimmer … and would become one of the world's best. Discover how faith, courage, and hard work led Jones to win an Olympic gold medal and set a new world record in his event. Find out what can happen when you overcome fear and strive to become all God calls you to be. Includes a personal note from Cullen Jones.

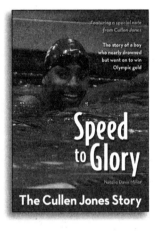

Available in stores and online!

Linspired, Kids Edition
The Jeremy Lin Story

Mike Yorkey and Jesse Florea

Linspired reveals the inside story of the remarkable and meteoric rise of Jeremy Lin, superstar of the New York Knicks, the first Asian-American-born player of Chinese/Taiwanese descent to play in the NBA. Discover the journey of the underdog who beat the odds to reach his current stardom and catch the attention of the sports world with both his in-credible basketball skills and his

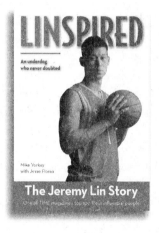

on and off-court example of faith, persistence, and hard work.

Available in stores and online!

Gifted Hands, Kids Edition: The Ben Carson Story

Gregg Lewis & Deborah Shaw Lewis

Ben Carson used to be the class dummy. Today he is one of the world's most brilliant surgeons.

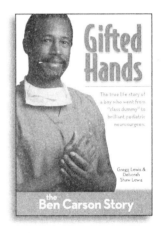

Gifted Hands, Kids Edition tells the extraordinary true story of an angry, young boy from the inner city who, through faith and determination, grew up to become one of the world's leading pediatric neurosurgeons. When Ben was in school, his peers called him the class dummy. But his mother encouraged him to succeed, and Ben discovered a deep love of learning. Ben found that anything is possible with trust and determination.

Toward the Goal: The Kaká Story

Jeremy V. Jones

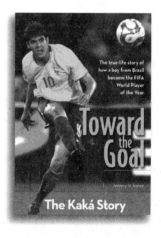

"I learned that it is faith that decides whether something will happen or not."

At the age of eight, Kaká already knew what he wanted in life: to play soccer and only soccer. He started playing in front of his friends and family, but when he suffered a crippling injury, doctors told him he would never play again. Through faith and perseverance Kaká recovered, and today he plays in front of thousands of fans every year. As the 2007 FIFA World Player of the Year and winner of the Ballon d'Or, this midfielder for Real Madrid has become one of the most recognized faces on the soccer field.

Available in stores and online!

Driven by Faith:
The Trevor Bayne Story

Godwin Kelly

Embracing the Race. Trevor Bayne is the youngest race car driver ever to win the Daytona 500. Throughout his high-speed career, from his early start driving go-karts to his incredible win at NASCAR's biggest race, Trevor attributes all his success to God—both on and off the track. His amazing story, from start to finish, will inspire young and old, racing enthusiasts or not, as they read *Driven by* 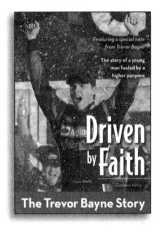 *Faith*, the story of a boy unafraid to share his faith, and a man who gives all the glory to God. Includes a personal note from Trevor Bayne.

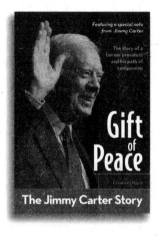

We want to hear from you. Please send your comments about this book to us in care of zreview@zondervan.com. Thank you.

ZONDERVAN.com/
AUTHORTRACKER
follow your favorite authors